German Tanks
& Fighting Vehicles
of World War II

CHARTWELL
BOOKS INC.

in association with Phoebus

Written by Chris Ellis and Peter Chamberlain
Illustrated by John Batchelor
Edited by Bernard Fitzsimons
Compiled by Ian Close

Published by Chartwell Books Inc
A Division of Book Sales Inc
110 Enterprise Avenue
Secaucus, New Jersey 07094

Library of Congress Catalog
Card Number 76-14637

This edition © 1976
Phoebus Publishing Company
BPC Publishing Limited
169 Wardour Street, London W1A 2JX
This material first appeared in Purnell's History
of the World Wars Specials © 1975
Phoebus Publishing Company

ISBN 0 7026 0011 3

Peter Chamberlain and **Chris Ellis** have collaborated
on a large number of publications and are widely recognised as leading experts in the weapon and fighting
vehicle field. Peter Chamberlain is a consultant to the
Imperial War Museum.

John Batchelor, after serving in the RAF, worked in the
technical publications departments of several British
aircraft firms, and went on to contribute on a freelance
basis to many technical magazines. Since then his work
for Purnell's Histories of the World Wars and Purnell's
World Wars Specials has established him as one of the
most outstanding artists in his field.

ABOUT THIS BOOK

When Germany went to war in 1939, she had the most professional and modern army in the world. Pride of place belonged to the Panzer divisions, the embodiment of a radically new concept of warfare – the *Blitzkrieg.* The Panzer division was designed as a highly mobile, self-contained fighting force, capable of smashing through the enemy's defences, creating confusion and, finally, collapse. To achieve these aims each division was equipped with a formidable range of fighting vehicles.

This book tells the story of those fighting vehicles – from the secret training machines of the Weimar period, through the intense innovative and experimental phase, to World War II itself.

From the lightest four-wheeled armoured car to the heaviest tank and self-propelled gun, the vehicles are analysed, model by model. The text provides a wealth of fascinating and comprehensive information while the illustrations – skilfully drawn and in full colour – add the necessary visual impact.

CONTENTS

ARMOURED CARS
REICHSWEHR RUNABOUTS

The early German victories of the Second World War were achieved largely through the bold use of fighting vehicles, closely supported by aerial bombardment, to bypass enemy fortifications, isolate his forces and attack his nerve centres. But the finely honed Panzer Divisions that shattered Poland, France and – for a while – Russia, had their roots in the *Reichswehr*'s early experiments with armoured cars – the 'paper panzers' of the 1920s and early 1930s

Armoured cars played a more important part in the development of armoured doctrine in Germany in the years between the two world wars than in any other major military power. This was largely due to the severe restrictions imposed by the Versailles Treaty of 1919, which prohibited tanks in the small new post-war German army (the *Reichswehr*) but permitted a number of armoured cars for police and patrol work.

In the First World War the Germans trailed way behind the British in the development of armoured cars and by the time of the Armistice in 1918 had only a token number of types in service. Erhardt were the main builders, and 20 new Erhardt vehicles were, in fact, the first armoured cars to see service with the *Reichswehr*. Some 30 armoured lorries were also pressed into service to help the new Republic's police and army to deal with the smouldering civil unrest of 1919.

A further stopgap type was a conversion of the First World War Daimler KD I four-wheel drive artillery tractor to make quite an effective armoured car. This was thus one of the earliest of all four-wheel drive armoured vehicles, known as the *Panzerkraftwagen* Daimler DZVR (*Daimler-Zugmaschine mit Vier Radantrieb*, or four-wheel drive Daimler tractor). Less than 50 of them were converted to armoured cars with a simple armoured box body with side doors.

The Versailles Treaty conditions were imposed from January 1920 under the aegis of the Allied Control Commission. By late 1920 the *Reichswehr* had organised seven motor transport battalions, each of which was allowed by the Commission to have 15 armoured personnel carriers – 105 armoured vehicles in all.

Dummy armoured cars used for training by the Reichswehr, on parade in 1933. Inset: An earlier type, with the body mounted on a tricycle

Bundesarchiv

The resulting vehicle was again based on the Krupp-Daimler KD I, but the chassis was improved to allow all the wheels to be of the same diameter (the DZVR had rear wheels bigger than the front as in the original tractor). No armament or cupola was permitted on the new vehicle – it merely had a box-like armoured body with loopholes, and provided seating for 12 men in addition to the three-man crew. Known as the *Gepanzerter Mannschaftstransportwagen*, SdKfz 3 (armoured personnel carrier, special vehicle 3) it was the forerunner of the many armoured cars and troop carriers that were to see service with the German forces up to the end of the war.

The SdKfz 3 had four-wheel drive and solid tyres, weighed a little under 11 tons and was 20 ft long; top speed was 31 mph and it had 11 mm of armour. Though of limited tactical value – the cross-country performance was poor – these vehicles remained in service well into the 1930s, some becoming radio-fitted command vehicles when more modern armoured cars were available in large numbers.

The other type of armoured car built in the early 1920s was the so-called *Schutzpolizei Sonderwagen* (protection police special vehicle). It was intended for internal security duties and was a much more effective vehicle than the SdKfz 3. The state police numbered 150,000 men and the Versailles Treaty allowed one car for every thousand. However, only about 104 were actually made, three different types built by Daimler, Erhardt, or Benz. They were generally similar to the SdKfz 3 but had twin turrets with machine-gun, a cupola, and rear steering as well as front steering. They were built and placed in service between 1920 and 1923, and in the 1930s some were taken over by the *Reichswehr*. Later, a few were converted as armoured transport vehicles for high ranking Nazis and used as such in the Second World War. In the 1920s however, they served the police, 72 with the Prussian state police and 32 with other states.

Gathering momentum

In the meantime the Army was becoming more ambitious, and in the latter half of the 1920s, under the leadership of General Hans von Seeckt, development of armoured vehicles for the *Reichswehr* took on a new momentum. A secret agreement was signed with Soviet Russia (the Rapallo Agreement) in 1926, under the terms of which the Soviets agreed to make available testing facilities for the Germans at Kazan on the Volga. This meant that some of the Versailles Treaty limitations preventing testing of prototypes on German soil would be circumvented.

The various existing armoured cars did not satisfy von Seeckt. He wanted the army to have vehicles suitable for reconnaissance and with a good cross-country performance under all conditions. The designation *Gepanzerter Mannschaftstransportwagen* was retained, however, since 'armoured troop carriers' were still within the Treaty limitations.

In 1926, *Heereswaffenamt Waffenprufamt* 6 (Army Armaments Weapons Testing Dept 6) responsible for the supply of vehicles, issued a new specification and invited manufacturers to submit prototypes for testing. These vehicles were to be certainly the most technically advanced wheeled cars ever developed at that time.

The specifications were extremely exacting, and included:
Six or more road wheels with multi-axle drive
Top road speed of 65 kmph and minimum road speed of 5 kmph
A distance of 200 km to be attainable for three successive days at average speed of 32 kmph
Ability to climb gradients of 1 in 3
Ability to cross trenches 1·5 m wide unaided
Wading ability to a depth of 1 m
Front and rear steering with equal performance in each direction, the changeover not to take more than ten seconds
Maximum turning circle of four times wheel base
Minimum engine noise
Chassis weight of maximum 4 tonnes and overall combat weight of maximum 7·5 tonnes
Ground clearance of 0·3 m
The vehicle to be able to run on standard gauge railway tracks without preparation
The ability to float without preparation, and a swimming speed of 5 kmph (later dropped)
A crew of five: commander, driver, first gunner, second gunner, radio-operator/rear driver.

The technical requirements also included very stiff specifications for engine, transmission and armour application.

So sophisticated were all these features that it was not possible to adapt any existing design. New and radical prototypes were needed and Daimler-Benz, Magirus and Büssing-NAG were finally selected to submit designs.

The Daimler-Benz model was an eight-wheeler, the ARW/MTM 1 (*Achtradwagen/ mannschaftstransportwagen* 1, or eight wheel vehicle/personnel carrier). This was one of the first designs to exercise the technical talents of Dr Ferdinand Porsche, whose many original ideas were later to make him famous both as a tank and car designer. All eight wheels on the Daimler were driven and it was of monocoque construction – a fairly novel idea for its day – with no conventional chassis. The front and rear pairs of wheels were steered and the four centre wheels turned as a group according to which end was steering. Water propulsion was achieved by a propeller and the hull was somewhat boat-shaped to facilitate the amphibious requirement. Two prototypes were built.

The Magirus design was an eight-wheeler similar to the Daimler but it does not appear to have been completed or delivered.

Büssing-NAG's design was even more complex, a ten-wheeler with all wheels independently suspended and with the two outer groups arranged in fours as steering bogies and the centre pair fixed. The steering wheel within the body was set on a vertical column and could be mounted into the steering box serving either end of the vehicle, depending on the direction of travel. Known as the ZRW (*Zehnradwagen* or ten-wheel vehicle) it had slab-sided additions to the basic boat-shaped superstructure.

The ZRW was not so successful as the Daimler eight-wheeler, being more unwieldy and – because of its central steering – having a less satisfactory degree of control. On amphibious trials the vehicle sank.

Officers consult their maps by an SdKfz 232 eight-wheeled radio-equipped armoured car

SIX-WHEELERS

The great financial slump of 1929–30, which affected Germany even more savagely than other major nations, saw the premature end of the ambitious and complex multi-wheel drive designs. It was clear that the high cost of such sophisticated vehicles would take up too much of the already limited defence budget and, at a conference held at the *Waffenprufamt* 6 offices in March 1930, the projects were reluctantly abandoned 'since the present financial status of the Reich makes vehicles of this size and type far too expensive'.

However, there was a fortuitous substitute, for in 1929 *Waffenprufamt* 6 had issued a requirement for a six-wheel military truck based on the production commercial 6×4 chassis built by the major truck factories. To meet this requirement Magirus had produced the M206, Büssing-NAG the G31 and Daimler-Benz the G3. A further suggestion put to the three manufacturers was the possibility of adding an armoured body to make a substitute armoured car to replace the abandoned eight- and ten-wheelers.

Daimler-Benz and Magirus were in the van of development – Daimler in particular being very successful with their G3 chassis. In 1929 an improved chassis, the G3a, was built. Daimler-Benz built the prototype armoured car in late 1929, using the G3 chassis, now known as the G-3(p) – for *panzerte* or armoured – with a faceted armoured body made by DeutschenWerke of Kiel. *Waffenprufamt* 6 had insisted on dual steering front and rear, but apart from this the layout of the vehicle betrayed its commercial truck origins. The water-cooled gasoline engine was at the front with drive to the rear axles, each of which had its own differential. The front axle steered from a normally positioned driving wheel, but there was an element of complication in providing the rear steering position, just forward of the rear axle, to steer the front

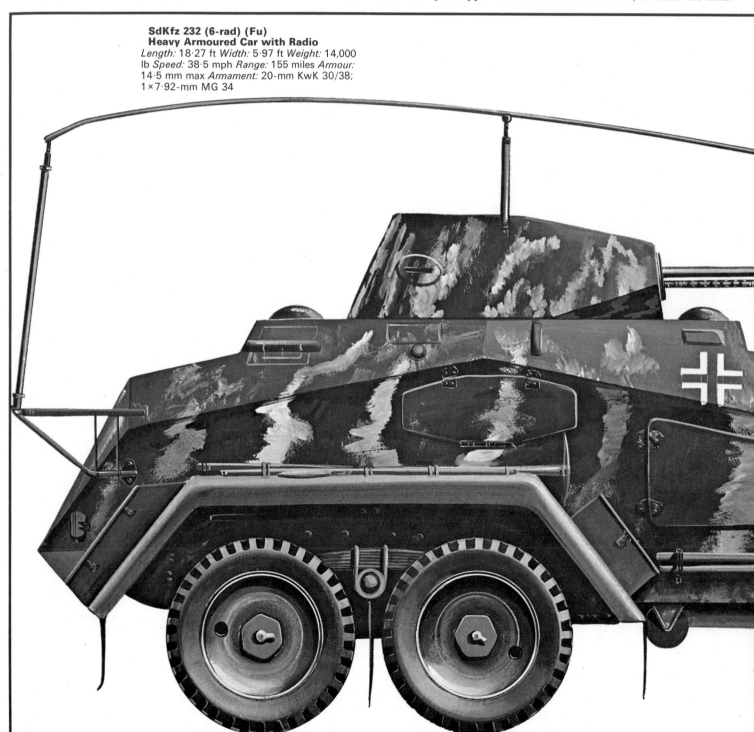

SdKfz 232 (6-rad) (Fu)
Heavy Armoured Car with Radio
Length: 18·27 ft *Width:* 5·97 ft *Weight:* 14,000 lb *Speed:* 38·5 mph *Range:* 155 miles *Armour:* 14·5 mm max *Armament:* 20-mm KwK 30/38; 1×7·92-mm MG 34

wheels. The multi-angled armoured superstructure followed the outline of a car, with a bonnet covering the front. There was a small turret on top with a 7·92-mm MG 13 machine-gun. The conventional chassis weighed 2·17 tons and the body weighed 2·26 tons, a total weight that made the fitting of large tyres essential. The gearbox was a commercial type with four forward and one reverse gear.

Trials of the prototype showed the need for a larger radiator and a stronger front axle, both of which were duly incorporated. One feature of the vehicle, which was to become a characteristic of later types also, was the canted steering wheel, slewed over on its column to reduce the overall height of the armoured superstructure by precious inches.

The first production vehicles, based on the Daimler-Benz G3a chassis, were delivered in 1932 and were used in the summer army exercises that year. Büssing-NAG delivered their first 12 vehicles to an externally similar design the following year. The full army designation for this armoured car was *Schwerer Panzerspähwagen* (sPzspähw) SdKfz 231 *mit Fahrgestell das Leichter Geländegängiger Lastkraftwagen (o)*, or, in English, heavy armoured reconnaissance vehicle type 231 on the chassis of the light cross-country truck (commercial). The short designation was SdKfz 231 (6-rad), the 6-rad (six-wheel) being added when eight-wheel vehicles appeared later. Basically, the vehicles had a simple girder type chassis, whose steering front axle had an additional linkage allowing them to be steered from a rear position. Semi-elliptic springs provided the suspension and a rubber loop type track or chains could be fitted round the rear pairs of wheels to give extra traction.

In 1934, Magirus-built vehicles of the same type appeared, but these differed in having side-mounted spare wheels which were free to revolve, thus aiding cross-country traction if the vehicle became bogged down.

Production of these six-wheelers ran to 1000 units by 1936 when they were superseded by a new eight-wheel design. The six-wheelers remained in service, however, and were still first-line equipment at the time of the invasions of Poland in September 1939 and of France in May 1940. Thereafter they disappeared rapidly and were used for training and internal security duties up to the end of the war.

There were actually three variants of the six-wheelers. The first, sPzspähw SdKfz 231 (6-rad), was the basic reconnaissance vehicle used by the heavy platoons of motorised reconnaissance battalions, and was popularly known as the *Waffenwagen*. The Daimler-built vehicle had a single 7·92-mm MG 34 machine-gun in its turret, but the Büssing and Magirus vehicle had a co-axial mount with a 20-mm KwK 30 or 38 plus one MG 34. These latter vehicles also had a mount on the turret roof for carrying another MG 34 for anti-aircraft defence.

Commanders' vehicles

The sPzspähw (Fu) – for *Funkwagen* or radio vehicle – SdKfz 232 was the model used by unit commanders. It was based on either the Magirus or Büssing chassis and had the co-axial turret mount with 20-mm gun. A curved 'bedstead' frame aerial on the same axis as the body and attached by poles to the rear superstructure was the characteristic feature of this vehicle. An ingenious front support in the shape of a shallow 'U' was pivoted on the turret top, thus allowing the turret to traverse without hindrance from the top hamper of the aerial. A 100-watt radio for communications with the rear was fitted in this vehicle.

The sPzFuWg (*Schwerer Panzerfunkwagen*) SdKfz 263 was superficially similar to the SdKfz 232, but actually it differed in many ways. It was intended in the first place as an armoured command vehicle for a higher formation commander or his staff, and the turret was fixed in the forward position. The frame aerial was larger than that of the SdKfz 232 and was fixed, but had provision for being lowered. The vehicle lacked the 20-mm gun and had only an MG 34 in the turret front, with no AA machine-gun. When used as a mobile headquarters, a separate pole radio mast which was carried in sections in the vehicle could be erected on the ground. Lacking turret traverse gear, the vehicle had more internal space, allowing room for a staff officer's map board and a radio-operator and wireless gear to be carried.

There was only one other contemporary six-wheel armoured car in German service at this period. This was the SdKfz 247 (6-rad), which in German military terminology was the *Schwerer Gepanzerter Personenkraftwagen auf Fahgestell des Leichter Geländegängiger Lastkraftwagen (o)* (heavy armoured personnel carrier on the chassis of the light cross-country lorry). This vehicle was of little significance and was essentially the chassis of the Krupp L2H 143 6×4 1·5-ton truck with an armoured body. It had no turret or armament, and the few built between 1936 and 1938 were used as command or observation vehicles for high-ranking officers in the early parts of the Second World War. The sloped armour body was similar in style to that of the SdKfz 231 (6-rad) six-wheeler.

An SdKfz 231 six-wheeled heavy armoured car, used during the invasions of Poland and France

Bundesarchiv

FOUR-WHEELERS

In the meantime, the limitations imposed by the defence budget and the Versailles Treaty had combined to push armoured car development in Germany in a new and more realistic direction. In order to train an army officially deprived of tanks in tank warfare, it was necessary to find some substitute for actual tanks.

In a 1928 military exercise a commercial truck was disguised to look like a tank, and the success of this idea led *Waffenprufamt 6* to have some *Panzernachbildung* (simulated armoured fighting vehicles) made up for use on a more extensive scale. Made of wood or card outline, the earliest of these 'paper panzers' were simply sectional dummy tank bodies fitted round the Hanomag or BMW Dixi light cars then in military service.

In 1930 a standardised design was introduced, this time for a simulated armoured car, which featured an aluminium body on an Adler Standard 6 car chassis. Later, thin sheet steel was used. The Adler had a dummy rotating turret and carried a full crew of commander, gunner, radio-operator, and driver. (This idea proved so successful that dummy armoured cars and tanks were used for training up to the end of the Second World War, thus releasing valuable fighting vehicles for service.)

Having built a dummy armoured car on the Adler Standard 6 chassis, the next logical step was to use this readily available 4 × 2 chassis as the basis for an actual armoured car, resulting in the Kfz 13 series which were designated as *Mittlerer Gepanzerter Personenkraftwagen* (medium armoured passenger car). The requirement for this vehicle was issued in 1932, and it entered service in 1934, remaining in use into the early 1940s. Daimler headed the production consortium. The vehicle betrayed its motor car ancestry in its front engine layout and conventional leaf spring suspension. A radio/command version was also produced, the Kfz 14.

Basic weapons carrier

The Kfz 13 was a *Waffenwagen* (weapons carrier) for reconnaissance units, open-topped and very basic. The vehicle had a 3 litre 6-cylinder engine with four-speed gearbox, and the lightly armoured superstructure (5 mm to 8 mm) was welded. The semi-elliptic spring suspension was of the motor car type. The armament was an MG 34 on a pedestal mount with a light front shield. Internally, the vehicle retained a normal motor car style of layout. The Kfz 14 differed in carrying a radio set with a frame aerial which could be lowered when not required. Kfz 14s had no gun and always accompanied Kfz 13s since the latter lacked any kind of signalling facilities.

While excellent for training, both the Kfz 13 and Kfz 14 were patently below any minimum combat standard. They were too lightly armoured to withstand even small arms fire, the cross-country performance was severely limited, and they were rather unstable due to the high centre of gravity imposed by the armoured body. Even so, Kfz 13s were still in service as late as 1943 on the Russian front because of shortages of later

types. Thus, though to a large extent the Kfz 13 and 14 were expedients, they were important in enabling troops to familiarise themselves with the use and deployment of armoured cars. They saw their widest use in the Polish campaign of 1939, the occupation of Czechoslovakia earlier that year and the invasion of France in 1940.

In 1936, when re-armament was fully under way in Germany, there came the adoption of a number of *Einheits* (standard) chassis which were to serve as the basis for all new wheeled vehicle designs. Among them was the *Einheitsfahrgestell I für Schwerer Personenkraftwagen* (standard chassis model 1 for heavy passenger cars) which had a rear-mounted engine and was intended specifically for armoured car use. (*Einheitsfahrgestell II* was similar but had a front-mounted engine and was used for conventional military vehicles of the personnel carrier or *Kübelwagen* type.)

Most of the requirements originally laid down for armoured cars were built into the specification, albeit in a less exacting form, and there was an additional demand for maximum standardisation of components throughout the *Einheitsfahrgestell* range. The motor industry had to design new chassis to meet all these requirements as existing ones were not robust enough. Chassis prototypes were displayed at the 1936 Berlin Motor Show, and the first armoured cars on this chassis, intended to replace the Kfz 13 and 14, appeared in service the following year.

The full designation was *Leichter Panzerspähwagen mit Einheitsfahrgestell I für Schwerer Personenkraftwagen* (light armoured reconnaissance car with the standard chassis model 1 for the heavy passenger car). The original requirement was for a *Waffenwagen* with a single machine-gun, but this was later changed to a 20-mm tank gun, and a radio car for command and communication use. In fact there were several variations, the most important models being:

Leichter Panzerspähwagen(MG) (SdKfz 221) *mit 7·92-mm MG 34*.

Leichter Panzerspähwagen (SdKfz 221) *mit 28-mm sPzD 41.* (This was a Second World War period conversion of the original model with a tapered bore anti-tank rifle.)

SdKfz 221 Light Armoured Car (opposite)
Length: 15·7 ft *Width:* 6·4 ft *Weight:* 8820 lb
Speed: 50 mph *Range:* 185 miles *Armour:*
14·5 mm max *Armament* 1 x 28-mm

Kfz 13 Adler Armoured Car
Length: 13·8 ft *Width:* 5·6 ft *Weight:* 4850 lb
Speed: 37 mph *Range:* 200 miles *Armour:* 8 mm
max *Armament:* 1 × 7·92-mm MG 34

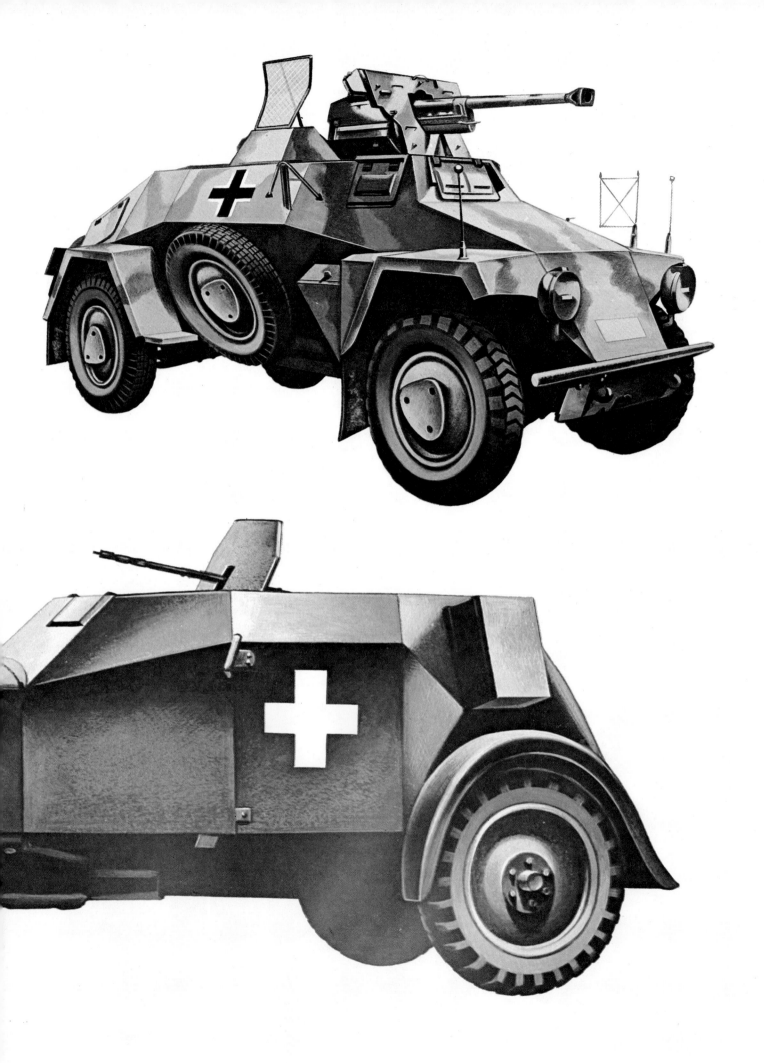

Leichter Panzerspähwagen (20-mm) (SdKfz 222). (This model had the 20-mm KwK tank gun to meet the revised *Waffenwagen* requirement.)

Leichter Panzerspähwagen (Fu) (SdKfz 223). (This model was radio equipped to meet the original *Funkwagen* requirement.)

Kleiner Panzerfunkwagen (SdKfz 260). (This was a specialised radio car development with more extensive equipment, intended for use by HQ units for communication on divisional or regimental networks. Its turret was set further back than on the 223 and it rarely carried a machine-gun.)

Kleiner Panzerfunkwagen (SdKfz 261). (This model was a later development of SdKfz 260 and was externally similar, but mechanical changes gave it a slightly better cross-country performance.)

All models in the SdKfz 221/222 series were based on a Horch/Auto-Union chassis (built by Horch-Werke of the Auto-Union combine) and Eisenwerk Westerhutte was the parent firm of the production contractors. Production in 1936–38 was on the Ausf (model) A chassis which had a 3·5 litre 75-hp engine, and 1939–42 production was on the Ausf B chassis with a 3·8 litre 81-hp engine. Production ceased in 1942 but these useful little vehicles remained in service for the duration of the war and the layout and style had some influence on British, French and Russian light armoured car design from 1940 onwards.

The chassis had four-wheel drive, fully independent suspension, optional four wheel steering (later this was dispensed with), and a self-locking differential which ensured both wheels on each side received power whatever the ground conditions. The hull was of welded armour plate, had a door each side, hinged visors front and rear, and a hand-turned turret traversed from the gun mounting. The turret was open-topped in the case of the SdKfz 221, seven-sided in

the SdKfz 221 and ten-sided in the SdKfz 222. Hinged wire-mesh screens on top were intended to deflect grenades.

The chassis proved to be very complex to build and hard to maintain, and this led to the early demise of the *Einheitsfahrgestell I*, for once the conditions of war had shown up the problems of both maintaining an increased production rate and keeping vehicles in service, there was a move to further rationalise chassis production. Since production of the *Einheitsfahrgestell I* chassis ceased in 1942, output of SdKfz 221 series armoured cars ended accordingly. Under the Schell programme, which sought to reduce and simplify the available range of military chassis from 1942, four-wheel chassis were discontinued, and all new armoured cars were big eight-wheelers.

The hulls were all welded as were the turrets when fitted. Cross-country performance of the vehicle was good, and armour protection was 14·5 mm at the front and 5–8 mm elsewhere. Weight was between 3·8 and 4·8 tons according to type.

In general the SdKfz 221 replaced the Kfz 13 in motorised reconnaissance units from 1936. Various other types of unit, including tank battalions, also procured these vehicles, sometimes for liaison work.

SdKfz 222 Light Armoured Car
Length: 15·7 ft *Width:* 6·4 ft *Weight:* 10,580 lb *Speed:* 50 mph *Range:* 185 miles *Armour:* 14·5 mm max *Armament:* 1 × 20-mm; 7·92-mm MG 34

Artillery units used them as mobile observation posts, but the major users were the reconnaissance companies of armoured reconnaissance battalions.

The SdKfz 221 was armed with only an MG 34 in the front of its small turret. A number of them were refitted with 20-mm tapered bore anti-tank guns, set high in the turret, the front of which was cut down, but this was not a widespread conversion as the importance of these small armoured cars decreased as the war progressed – most 20-mm tapered bore guns were fitted to other types, like half-tracks.

The SdKfz 222 with its 20-mm KwK 30 or 38 gun in the turret came into service from 1938. It differed from the SdKfz 221 in that it had a limited range radio set (the 221 had no communications gear), and a more prominently cut-away rear superstructure to give the driver a better rear view when reversing. The turret of the 222 was larger than that of the 221, having ten sides, and accommodated the 20-mm automatic gun adapted from an aircraft gun. It had a ten-shot magazine and could fire either armour-piercing or high explosive rounds.

The gun had a high rate of fire (1280 rpm in the KwK 30 or 480 rpm in the KwK 38). The high angle of elevation (87°) enabled the gun to be used against aircraft. A hand-wheel controlled both elevation and traverse, with a linking arm to traverse the turret with the mount. Two smoke projectors on each side of the turret supplemented the gun, and an MG 34 was co-axial with the 20-mm weapon.

The turret was fairly constricted, despite its increased size; the commander was also the gunner and the other crew members were the driver and the radio-operator, who also acted as loader. The KwK 38 gun had increased elevation and was fitted to the later production vehicles. The SdKfz 222, with its heavy armament, mainly equipped

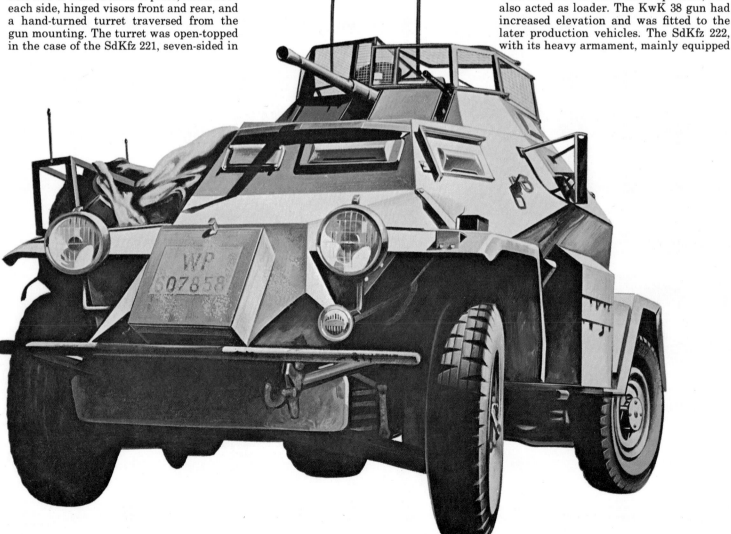

the divisional reconnaissance units. The top speed was 50 mph and the radius of action was 110 miles in cross-country conditions.

The SdKfz 222 had a shorter run of service than most. Because of the very severe terrain on the Russian Front in 1941–42, these small four-wheel vehicles proved not entirely suitable for the divisional reconnaissance role, and they were largely replaced from 1942 by the SdKfz 250/9 half-track which was fitted with the turret from SdKfz 222.

The SdKfz 223 radio car came into service in 1938 and was a replacement for the Kfz 14. It had a small turret similar to that of the SdKfz 221, and a prominent frame-type radio aerial mounted on the hull. This could be collapsed on its pylons if desired to reduce the overall height and aid concealment. This aerial was rather cumbersome, and later models simply had a sectionalised pole aerial which was easier to handle. The SdKfz 223 was a companion vehicle to the 221 in the reconnaissance companies of armoured reconnaissance battalions.

The *Kleiner Panzerfunkwagen* (small armoured radio vehicle) SdKfz 260 and 261 were expressly designed for use by unit and formation commands, with radio suitable for maintaining divisional and regimental links. They had a more cut-away superstructure at the rear as in the 222, and the small turret was set further back to allow more room inside the hull for radio equipment. Though both vehicles in theory carried MG 34, in practice the armament was usually omitted due to the great encumbrance of the signals equipment.

The different designations for the SdKfz 260 and 261 were mainly to account for their different radio outfits. The 260 had only sectionalised pole aerials, usually carried with the lower sections rigged. Early models of the SdKfz 261 had the big frame aerial, but this was later replaced by pole aerials.

An SdKfz 223 armoured reconnaissance vehicle of Guderian's Panzergruppe *in France, August 1940*

SdKfz 261 Light Armoured Car
Length: 15·58 ft *Width:* 6·5 ft *Weight:* 9500 lb
Speed: 50 mph *Range:* 200 miles *Armour:* 8 mm
Armament: nil

One last light armoured car model in the same 'family' of four-wheelers was the SdKfz 247, produced in very small numbers on the *Einheitsfahrgestell II* chassis, which was the alternative passenger car chassis for the *Einheits* series, differing from the *Einheitsfahrgestell I* by having front engine and transmission rather than a rear engine. The manufacturer was again Auto-Union/Horch. This chassis was used for the big series of standard cross-country cars produced by the Germans and the SdKfz 247 – not to be confused with the different SdKfz 247 (6-rad) already described – had an armoured body in place of an open car body.

This vehicle was classed as an armoured personnel carrier, and some were issued to reconnaissance units. In the main they went to elite fighting units like Panzer Division Gross Deutschland or were used as personnel transport by formation staffs and commanders. There were actually two models: the SdKfz 247/I was the original version, while the other, SdKfz 247/II, had a more powerful radio set and a thicker front armour shield. A prominent 'star' aerial was a feature of this later model.

Light armoured cars were proved early on to be highly suited to the reconnaissance role, hence the subsequent designation of *Panzerspähwagen* (armoured reconnaissance car) for this type of vehicle. By the time the first Panzer Divisions were formed in 1938, three armoured recce companies with motor cycles and light armoured cars were organic to each division. In a Panzer Division there were 42 cars of various types with the three companies, and a further eight cars with the recce company of the division's mechanised infantry regiment. The reconnaissance company of an Infantry Division had three light armoured cars, intended for command and communication use. The recce company of a Motorised Division included 18 light armoured cars.

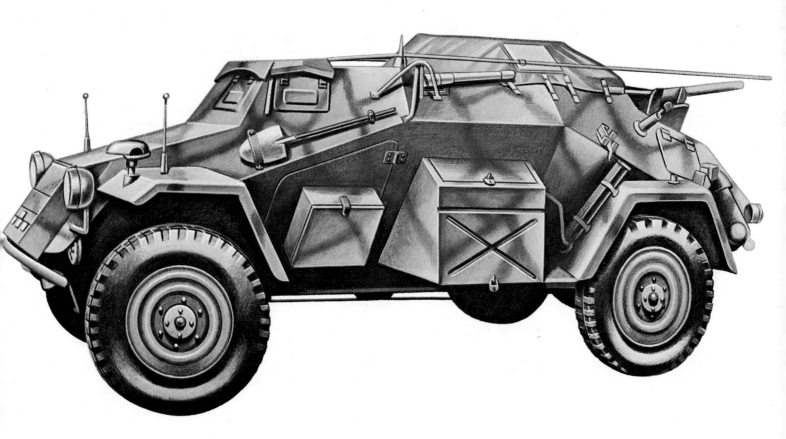

EIGHT-WHEELERS

By far the most important of all German armoured cars in the Second World War were the impressive eight-wheelers which were originally conceived as heavy cars to complement the light four-wheelers. The origin of the eight-wheelers goes back to 1934 when *Waffenprufamt* 6 asked Büssing-NAG to develop an experimental eight-wheel chassis with all wheels driven and with steering on all axles. This was at the time when the *Einheits* series of cross-country chassis was being evolved to cover all weight chassis. It was the 'light' *Einheitsfahrgestell* which formed the basis for both the standard light cross-country personnel carrier and the light armoured cars of the SdKfz 221 series. The eight-wheel chassis design was very complex and the idea of a cross-country truck version was never pursued. However, it was decided to develop an armoured car on this chassis, and in 1935 the Ministry of War funded a prototype, known as VsKfz (*Versuchkraftfahrzeuge* or experimental vehicle) 623.

A production design was finalised and a preliminary order placed, the intention being to replace the rather unsatisfactory six-wheelers then in service. First deliveries took place in 1937 and by 1940 the various types of eight-wheeler were in widespread service. The initial types were intended as direct replacements for the existing six-wheelers and for this reason they took exactly the same ordnance numbers, but to differentiate between the old and new the number of wheels was indicated with the designation. Thus the old model SdKfz 231 (6 rad) was replaced by the SdKfz 231 (8 rad). Both the old and new models were in service concurrently, moreover, especially between 1938 and 1940. The basic eight-wheeler chassis was of sturdy two-section girder construction with tubular cross members. It was actually light for the size of the vehicle, but the long armoured body gave extra rigidity. A Büssing-NAG V8 gasoline engine of 155 bhp was mounted at the rear of the vehicle which was actually the front of the chassis – the chassis and body were reversed in relation to each other and there was no front and rear in the conventionally accepted sense. The gearbox was mounted centrally on the chassis, the wheels were mounted in fours on two bogies, all independently sprung, and also linked in pairs with semi-elliptic springs. All axles steered and there was a reduction gear box for each bogie. There were six gears available in either direction, an auxiliary high/low ratio being available with its own gear lever. Steering and driving controls were duplicated for driving in either direction. A special differential in each of the gear reduction boxes compensated for the differing turning radii of the inner and outer pairs of wheels. Simple pressed-steel disc wheels were fitted, with low-pressure self-sealing cross-country tyres. The entire design was well thought out and extremely advanced for its time.

The first vehicle type produced on the eight-wheel chassis, the SdKfz 231 (8-rad), followed the pattern of previous output in being a *Waffenwagen*. It had a turret mounting the 20-mm KwK 30 or 38 automatic cannon, with a co-axial MG 34, both fired by foot pedal. The four man crew consisted of a gunner, commander, driver and second driver/radio-operator.

Unlike the earlier types, the eight-wheeler was quite a roomy vehicle with good stowage arrangements. The welded hull was of face-hardened armour, 15 mm thick on the turret front, 8–10 mm elsewhere on vertical or near vertical faces, and 5 mm on sloped faces such as the glacis, although later production vehicles, built after combat experience, had the armour maximum increased to 30 mm. The very earliest vehicles had a front stowage basket on the nose with a forward face 10 mm thick, which acted effectively as spaced armour, giving extra frontal protection. Late production vehicles with 30 mm of armour were of course slightly heavier, and the engine was bored out to give 180 bhp, and thus an increased performance to compensate for the added weight.

Spacious turret

The turret of the SdKfz 231 was a roomy hexagonal structure. The commander was provided with a seat on the left-hand side, with a folding periscope which had provision for a camera attachment to photograph the terrain on reconnaissance work. There was a ball race for turret traverse with a combined traverse and gun elevating wheel with the gunner on the right and a more highly geared over-ride control for the commander. Seats and other fittings were attached to the turret sides and there was thus no turret floor. Vision ports in the sides and an opening roof hatch were other features of the turret.

The SdKfz 231 formed the backbone of the divisional armoured reconnaissance battalions in increasing numbers from 1937–38, and by late 1940 had completely supplanted the SdKfz 231 (6-rad) in first line units. As with the earlier types of car, there was a companion, radio-fitted car for the use of commanders (though the SdKfz 231 (8-rad) also had a wireless set). The special radio-fitted vehicle was the SdKfz 232 (Fu) (8-rad). This *Funkwagen* variant was in most respects similar to the SdKfz 231 (8-rad) except that it had a large frame aerial above the turret, as on the 6-rad version. A shaped pivoting front support allowed the turret to traverse without disturbing the aerial frame. The aerial was cumbersome and vulnerable, so on later production models the frame aerial was replaced by a sectionalised rod aerial which could be erected on the turret roof, and a star-shaped aerial which fitted on the rear decking. The SdKfz 232 (Fu) (8-rad) again was armed with the MG 34 and 20-mm gun in the turret.

Once again there was a special command vehicle for signals staff and headquarters use which in this case dispensed with the turret and was given special bodywork. It had a full-width superstructure replacing the turret and carried 100-watt or 80-watt medium wave radio equipment to maintain battalion, regimental and divisional links. Designated SdKfz 263 (8-rad), this was known as a *Schwerer Panzerfunkwagen*

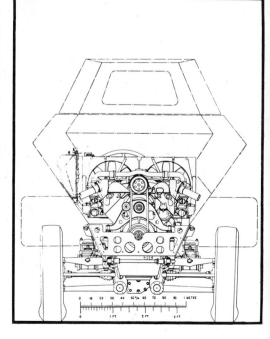
An SdKfz 231 (8-rad) heavy armoured car

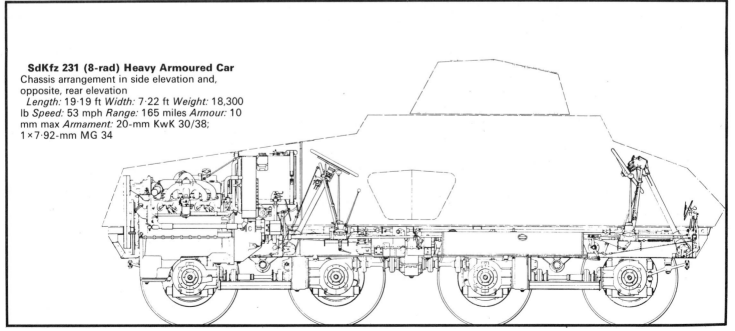

SdKfz 231 (8-rad) Heavy Armoured Car
Chassis arrangement in side elevation and,
opposite, rear elevation
  Length: 19·19 ft *Width:* 7·22 ft *Weight:* 18,300
lb *Speed:* 53 mph *Range:* 165 miles *Armour:* 10
mm max *Armament:* 20-mm KwK 30/38;
1 × 7·92-mm MG 34

rather than a *Panzerspähwagen*. The superstructure followed the angles of the lower hull sides and there were access hatches on the roof. The only armament was a ball-mounted MG 34 in the hull front. A large frame bedstead aerial was mounted above the superstructure but, as with other radio vehicles, it was replaced by a sectionalised rod aerial on later vehicles. From the end of 1941 this type of vehicle went out of production, its function being undertaken by radio-equipped half-tracks. The SdKfz 263 (8-rad) served with signals platoons of armoured reconnaissance battalions as well as some formation commands. It weighed 8·5 tons fully laden, rather more than the standard *Waffenwagen*.

These were the main armoured cars in service when the great German campaigns of 1939–40 took place. At this period the armoured reconnaissance companies and battalions, equipped with motor cycle and armoured car platoons, were in the forefront of the attack, playing an important part. From late 1941 onwards, however, the importance of armoured cars and the German reconnaissance troops declined. This was mainly because the German forces were forced largely on to the defensive in Europe, while in the Western Desert and on the Russian Front the half-track could undertake most of the functions of the armoured car, and other roles besides, particularly those of a defensive nature. Conversely, the Allies, who went on to the offensive, began to turn out more and more armoured cars, using them up to 1944 and 1945 – by which time they had almost disappeared from German service.

The changing needs of the German army are reflected in the first armoured car to depart from the established order. This was the *Schwerer Panzerspähwagen* 75-mm SdKfz 233, introduced for armoured reconnaissance units, which needed to be able to provide their own mobile fire support.

The gun was the well-tested 75-mm low velocity KwK 37 L/24 which had been used on the earlier PzKpfw IV tanks and various types of assault gun. It was mounted on the vehicle in the front of the superstructure, and both the turret and hull top as fitted to the SdKfz 231 (8-rad) were omitted, and replaced by low superstructure side additions, leaving the vehicle open-topped. The gun could fire smoke, high explosive and two types of armour-piercing round, a total of 55 rounds of all types being carried. The crew was reduced to three men – driver, rear driver/radio-operator and gunner/commander. The gun had very limited traverse and was aimed via a simple dial sight.

Protracted development

The status of armoured cars in the German forces is demonstrated by the time taken to get the final generation of eight-wheelers into service. A start was made in August 1940 to replace the eight-wheeler with an improved version. Externally the new vehicle appeared similar to the original Büssing-NAG design, but one major difference was that it had a monocoque hull instead of a separate chassis. The same type of eight-wheel steering was employed, but the bogies were attached directly to the lower hull. Büssing-NAG undertook design and construction, while Deutschen produced the hull, which was similar to that of the preceding series of eight-wheelers, but was much simplified. The two separate groups of mudguards that covered the wheels on the earlier models were replaced by new one-piece mudguards with integral stowage boxes.

A prime requirement for the new design was that it should operate well at extremes of climate, particularly in tropical climates. The Czech firm of Tatra was given the task of developing a high-powered engine to replace the gasoline engine, and a compact V-12 14·8 litre unit was evolved.

The prototype did not appear until July 1941, by which time German troops were fighting in North Africa, and the complicated Tatra engine proved too noisy for desert operations. It was rejected and an improved engine designed with the major aim of muffling the noise. By this time (late 1942), operations in North Africa were not going well, and priority was being given to tanks and assault guns, so progress on the new armoured car was slow.

In the event it did not enter production until 1943, and did not see service in any numbers until 1944. Armour thickness of 30 mm at the front was standard with 14 mm and 10 mm on other faces. Increased fuel capacity was a major feature of this vehicle, giving a range of 370 miles against the 170 miles of the earlier eight-wheelers. Later vehicles had even greater capacity, increasing the range to 620 miles. Around 2300 of this new series were built from 1944 up to March 1945, and the model, designated SdKfz 234, received an unexpected new lease of life when it was selected for increased production (100 vehicles a month) in the closing weeks of the war. This was largely because it was relatively simple for the hard pressed bomb-damaged factories to build as the military situation deteriorated. The scheme was something of a last ditch stand which never really materialised. Designated ARK by the manufacturers, the new eight-wheeler was built in several forms.

The basic *Waffenwagen* version had the usual 20-mm KwK 38 automatic gun and was designated *Schwerer Panzerspähwagen* (20-mm) SdKfz 234/1. The KwK 38 was arranged in an open-top six-sided turret, with high elevation (75°) making it suitable for engaging air targets. Folding mesh panels on top of the turret prevented

SdKfz 232 (8-rad) (Fu)
Heavy Armoured Car with Radio
Length: 19·19 ft *Width:* 7·22 ft *Weight:* 19,400 lb *Speed:* 53 mph *Range:* 165 miles *Armour:* 10 mm max *Armament:* 20-mm KwK 30/38; 1 x 7·92-mm MG 34

grenades from being hurled inside. There was a co-axial 7·92-mm MG 42 in the mantlet. Some 20 spare ammunition magazines were carried and radio-telephone and wireless equipment fitted.

The excellence of the eight-wheel suspension on these cars made their cross-country performance almost equal to that of a tank and the road speed was, of course, much superior. The Soviet Army still used many light tanks (for example the T-70) in their reconnaissance units and the German Army decided that an armoured car capable of tackling a light tank at close range was a desirable asset, since early contact with enemy attacks was most often at reconnaissance unit level.

Thus was evolved possibly the best-known of all German armoured cars, the Puma, which was more fully designated *Schwerer Panzerspähwagen* (50-mm) SdKfz 234/2. This vehicle retained the basic ARK series eight-wheel chassis but had a new oval turret of very fine ballistic shape, with a 50-mm KwK 39/1 L/60 tank gun in a streamlined *Saukopf* (pig's head) mantlet. The turret had originally been developed for the Leopard light tank which had been

projected for the reconnaissance role in 1943–44 but had been abandoned at prototype stage. The 50-mm gun was very effective for its calibre, having semi-automatic action at a muzzle velocity of 2700 fps when firing armour-piercing ammunition. The compact mantlet included a recoil mechanism mounted above the gun, a telescopic sight, and a co-axial MG 42. Three smoke projectors were mounted as standard on each side of the turret.

The weight of the vehicle was of course increased by the addition of the turret, to 11·5 tons in combat order and 11·3 tons unladen. The mantlet armour was up to 100 mm thick, but armour elsewhere was as for the other eight-wheelers of the ARK type. The turret had full 360° traverse and the vehicle was fitted with radio-telephones as standard but could also carry long range Fu 12 radio equipment. The crew of four men remained as in the standard car and the commander had a periscope in the turret roof.

To supplement the Puma a more heavily armed support version of the armoured car was produced as a result of Hitler's personal intervention. Soviet armour packed a

powerful punch, and the idea of the additional vehicle, designated *Schwerer Panzerspähwagen* (75-mm) SdKfz 234/3, was to give support fire to the Puma. Basically the SdKfz 234/3 was an updated version of the SdKfz 233, with similar placing of the 75-mm KwK 51 L/24 low velocity gun. The vehicle was open-topped, the gun had a limited traverse and 55 rounds of ammunition were carried. The combat weight of this vehicle was 9·8 tons.

The SdKfz 234/3 was, of course, something of an expedient in common with a large number of late-war period German self-propelled guns. In this case the L/24 guns were plentifully available, having been removed from early versions of the PzKpfw IVs.

Still more illustrative of the expedient nature of the later German equipment was the final vehicle in the SdKfz 234 series, the *Schwerer Panzerspähwagen* (75-mm *lang*) SdKfz 234/4. This was yet another of the types suggested by Hitler and was potentially an excellent type, reflecting the desperate situation on Germany's fighting fronts in late 1944/early 1945.

The SdKfz 234/4 was in essence the same vehicle as the SdKfz 234/3, but instead of the short 75-mm gun of limited effect, the SdKfz 234/4 had the powerful long 75-mm Pak 40 anti-tank gun. This was a weapon of proven effectiveness as a ground mount, the standard anti-tank gun with infantry units. The SdKfz 234/4 simply took the complete gun and carriage, and placed it straight into the open fighting compartment of the SdKfz 234/3. The result was a crude but potent wheeled tank destroyer, with its traverse limited to that of the Pak 40 carriage. The wheels and trail were, of course, removed from the carriage but the gun shield was retained.

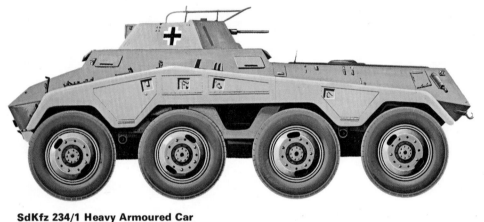

SdKfz 234/1 Heavy Armoured Car
Length: 19·72 ft *Width:* 7·74 ft *Weight:* 13,150 lb *Speed:* 53 mph *Range:* 370–620 miles *Armour:* 30 mm max *Armament:* 20-mm KwK 30/38; 1×7·92-mm MG 42

SdKfz 234/2 'Puma' Heavy Armoured Car
Length: 22·3 ft (inc gun) *Width:* 7·64 ft *Weight:* 25,880 lb *Speed:* 53 mph *Range:* 500–620 miles *Armour:* 40 mm max (100 mm on mantlet) *Armament:* 50-mm KwK 39/1; 7·92-mm MG 42

WH-1542940

The particular merit of the vehicle was its speed, low profile, and fast drive in either direction. Known to the troops as the *Pak-wagen* (anti-tank vehicle), it was intended to be built at a rate of 100 a month as a standard type. The chassis was well-proven, and relatively cheap, the gun was readily available and easy to fit. Its crudity did nothing to diminish its effectiveness – it could be turned out quickly and did all it was called upon to do. However, only a few were built, for in the closing months of the Second World War the entire system of production and procurement was in disarray and the promising *Pak-wagen* hardly got a chance to show its mettle.

Needless to say, these eight-wheel vehicles, well ahead of their time, have had much influence on subsequent armoured car development, and Britain, France, Holland and the Soviet Union, among other nations, have all produced multi-wheel drive vehicles which clearly owe something to the German designs that proved their worth in battle over several years of war.

The eight-wheelers did not exhaust German efforts at armoured car design, even though they represented the bulk of the output. Efforts were made continually during the war years to produce simpler four-wheel designs incorporating the lessons of battle.

Experimental vehicles

The *Mittlerer Panzerspähwagen* (medium armoured car) VsKfz 231 (4-rad) was an interesting vehicle which did not see production. Conceived in 1941, it was intended to be a four-wheel version of the eight-wheel SdKfz 231. The design also involved elements of the SdKfz 234, in that a six-cylinder Tatra air-cooled diesel engine was to be used. The VsKfz 231 had a shortened SdKfz 231 chassis, four wheels all driven, face-hardened armour of 30 mm frontal thickness and 8–14·5 mm elsewhere. The original idea was to have a 20-mm gun in a rotating turret, but this was changed to a 50-mm KwK 39. There was to be a co-axial MG 42 and a crew of four.

Büssing-NAG did the design work and Auto-Union/Horch were contracted to act as manufacturers. Orders for 1000 vehicles were placed, with production scheduled to start in October 1943. By the time plans had advanced this far, however, practical battle experience on the Russian Front had shown that half-tracks were more useful for reconnaissance work under the prevailing conditions and all work and production schedules on the car were cancelled.

Outside these activities came a whole series of prototypes for amphibious light armoured cars, built and designed by Hans Trippel, whose Trippelwerke factory had specialised in amphibious vehicle development before the war. Trippel made his prototypes as private ventures and never succeeded in having any designs adopted by the Wehrmacht, though they were tested and demonstrated. One major difficulty under war conditions was obtaining the necessary permission to carry out private venture work. However, in 1941 Trippel built an amphibious light personnel carrier similar in appearance to the famous Volkswagen *Schwimmwagen* – almost like a bathtub on wheels. Using this vehicle, the SG 6, as a basis, he built a light amphibious armoured car called the *Schildkrote* (Turtle), a prototype of which was ordered by the

German Army in January 1942. It had an Opel 2·5 litre motor car engine, was armed with an MG 81 and had a turret searchlight.

The demonstration was not successful when it took place in March 1942, but the following month Trippel secured orders for two prototypes with improved steering which were designated *Schildkrote II*. Tests were carried out using vanes fitted to the wheels to give propulsion in water, but eventually propeller drive via a power link to the engine was adopted. These new prototypes lacked turrets but were intended to have octagonal open-topped turrets rather like those of the SdKfz 222 series vehicles, and 20-mm cannon or 7·92-mm machine gun armament was proposed. Demonstrations of these new vehicles in the summer of 1942 were again unsuccessful. A third prototype, *Schildkrote III*, was then built, with the Tatra diesel engine developed for the VsKfz 231 (4-rad). Otherwise similar to the *Schildkrote II*, the *III* was also considered unsuitable.

However, all this led to Trippelwerke being engaged to undertake development work on a standard type of amphibious chassis with rear mounted Tatra engine, the E3 light armoured car and E3M munition carrier. These were built in 1944 and prototypes were demonstrated in October of that year. Due to the deteriorating war situation, however, there was no production order. The E3 was one of a projected series of *Einheits* vehicles which were part of a long term plan to produce a number of basic standardised vehicle types and thus reduce the dozens of different vehicles on the ordnance inventory.

The Germans supplemented their own vehicles with a number of captured types, though these saw service only in limited numbers. For instance, some armoured cars of French and Austrian origin were taken into service. The only type to see wide-scale service, however, was the French Panhard 178, which was taken into German service as the *Panzerspähwagen* P 204 (f), of which well over 150 were employed. This vehicle was conventional in appearance: a four-wheeler with central turret and a rear-mounted 105-hp two-stroke engine. Some were used on the Russian Front. They had a 25-mm Hotchkiss gun and co-axial machine-gun, with a maximum armour of 20 mm and a top speed of 50 mph.

One special adaptation of these cars was as railway patrol cars for the Russian Front. Fitted with flanged wheels, they were used to escort armoured trains and for fast patrol duties along the many miles of captured railway line used by the Wehrmacht for bringing supplies up to the fighting fronts. About 40 Panhards were so converted in early 1942.

One of the Austrian cars which saw service (as the SdKfz 254) was the Saurer RR7, designated by the Germans *Mittlerer Gepanzerter Beobachtungskraflwagen* (medium armoured observation vehicle). This was actually a wheel-cum-track vehicle that could change from wheels to track while in motion. It had a six-cylinder diesel engine and was intended for the Austrian Army as a light gun tractor. When Germany annexed Austria in 1938, the Germans ordered an armoured version and a small number were built and entered service in 1942. Another variation, with different fittings, saw even more limited service as a repair and maintenance vehicle. The SdKfz 254 was armed with only an MG 34.

A captured Panhard armoured car with German police badge takes part in an anti-partisan action with the Wehrmacht forces in Russia in 1941

SdKfz 234/3 Heavy Armoured Car (left)
Length: 19·68 ft (inc gun) *Width:* 7·64 ft *Weight:* 22,050 lb *Speed:* 53 mph *Range:* 370–620 miles *Armour:* 30 mm max *Armament:* 75-mm K 51

Keystone

CROSS-COUNTRY TRANSPORT

Armoured cars played a relatively minor part in German military activities during the Second World War, and a much more significant vehicle was the armoured half-track, which eventually took over many of the armoured car's roles. The half-track established a style for the use of armoured personnel carriers which is now an integral part of all major armies.

In fact, the idea of an armoured troop carrier was first exploited by Britain, for the thinking that led eventually to the development of tanks in Britain in 1915–16 stemmed from the need to carry infantry into action immune from machine-gun fire. The tank became an instrument of attack in its own right, but by 1918 the British had converted some to troop carriers – with sliding doors replacing the gun sponsons of Mk V tanks, or in the case of Mks V* and V** with lengthened hulls specially to carry troops. They were used as troop carriers not altogether successfully, at the Battle of Amiens in July 1918. The big Mk IX tank, known as the 'Pig' because of its ugly shape and bulk, was built, too late to see service, with ports for infantrymen to fire through from inside. It could also carry stores and equipment.

These efforts provided the British Army on the Western Front with a means of moving up infantry with a tank attack, and actually pre-dated by far similar German ideas. But with the coming of peace in 1918, these lessons were largely forgotten by the British who quickly reverted to what were virtually pre-war ideas. The poor economic condition of Britain was used, as always, as a convenient excuse to run down the Army and pack up development work.

Britain was not short of ideas, however, and an Experimental Mechanised Force was set up in the 1920s to study on a small scale the experiences of the last years of the Great War; they took one step further the idea of co-ordinated tank, infantry, assault engineers and artillery attack under one command – the basic principle of the Panzer Division in fact.

The leading British armoured warfare theorists were men who had been concerned with, or keen observers of, the development of armour in the First World War, among them Captain Liddell Hart and Generals Fuller and Swinton. Their writings on the subject were keenly followed in other nations, particularly in Germany. Liddell Hart, in particular, was a prolific writer and one of his prophetic statements in the 1920s was that 'motorised armed forces have to be able to perform similar feats to the marauding hordes of the Mongols'. Tactics demonstrated during exercises with Britain's Experimental Mechanised Force showed that it was possible to act as a 'marauding force' with fully mobile tanks, artillery and infantry breaking through conventional front lines, attacking or straddling lines of communication, operating against the enemy's undefended rear and so on.

But much of this work went unheeded in Britain, for by the 1930s the Experimental Mechanised Force has been disbanded and policy was switching back to older ideas: infantry walking into the attack behind slow-moving, machine-gun armed 'infantry tanks', barrages from prepared positions against fixed front lines and so on. The last vestiges of the 'marauding forces' idea were seen in 'cruiser tanks' and 'light tanks', the former to exploit the breakthrough made by the infantry, but acting largely independently. The nautical analogy in the classification did owe something to the writings of the pundits, but the essential ingredient of specialised infantry and artillery support was missing from British armoured doctrine in the 1930s.

Not so in Germany, however, where the German Army had the advantage of starting with a clean sheet, without preconceived ideas to obstruct innovations. As we have already seen, the idea of mechanised infantry was borne in mind from the start when the new *Reichswehr* formed seven motor battalions each with 15 armoured troop carriers. The seeds of the armoured half-track already existed in Germany.

French inspiration

The half-track idea was not, of course, German – it had been developed by Adolphe Kégresse, a French engineer who managed the Czar of Russia's personal motor fleet in the early 1900s. Kégresse had made a bogie assembly with rubber tracks to replace the back wheels of one of the Czar's cars, thus giving it superior traction in winter snow and ice. After the Russian Revolution of 1917, Kégresse returned to his native France and Citroën took up his half-track ideas with commercially successful results.

The French, British and American armies, among others, all had Citroën-Kégresse half-tracks in the 1920s and 1930s, but failed to exploit their full military potential. The British, in particular, had dropped half-tracks altogether by the late 1930s, though the US Army, under the impetus of war, went on to develop their own successful line of M3 series armoured half-tracks, derived directly from the simple Kégresse ideas. These American half-tracks proved to be among the most durable of military vehicles and many hundreds were still in service with the world's smaller armies (notably Israel) well into the 1970s, none of the surviving vehicles having been built later than 1945.

The first German half-track for military use was the Daimler-built Bremer Marienwagen. This appeared in 1917–18, and was basically a Daimler lorry with the body of an Erhardt armoured car. The back wheels were replaced by simple rubber-band type track units – and later one vehicle was built with track units replacing the front wheels also. Only four vehicles were built, and for various reasons, notably poor steering, uneasy control characteristics and track-shedding, the Bremer Marienwagen was abandoned. It was however designed as an armoured troop transport and would have been the German equivalent of the British troop-carrying tank. Various less significant prototypes had been built towards the end of the First World War, among them the Mannesman-Mulag *Panzerkraftwagen* an armoured lorry type of troop carrier with rifle ports, and the Daimler DZVR.

Half-track development took its most significant step forward in 1926, when the German War Ministry tested a number of available trucks and half-tracks to deter-

SdKfz 251/1 (opposite)
Medium Armoured Personnel Carrier
Length: 19·02 ft *Width:* 6·89 ft *Weight:* 8430 lb *Speed:* 34 mph *Range:* 185 miles *Armour:* 12 mm max *Armament:* 2 × 7·92-mm MG 34

'Mongol hordes': Panzer Grenadiers move in to attack a village from their SdKfz 251s

mine future procurement and operational policy. At the time there were several four-wheel drive tractors in production, built by firms like Kraus-Maffei, and some of these had 'add-on' half-track units similar to the basic Kégresse type (several manufacturers came up with their own half-track units, in the 1920s). A number of such vehicles were purchased, mainly as artillery tractors, and it was decided that for cross-country use efforts should be concentrated on this type of vehicle in future. Commercial output could not keep up with demand, however, and some rationalisation was needed. The other important point was that Hans von Seeckt, the Inspector of Mechanised Vehicles, realised that all arms would need to use half-track vehicles for cross-country transportation, not just the artillery.

By this time, moreover, the future structure of the German Army was being planned, and the deliberations led eventually to a requirement for prototypes in six weight classes. These, it was envisaged, would satisfy all the requirements of the various fighting arms. In 1932 contracts were placed with various automotive firms for trial vehicles.

All six prototypes were built and tested, and in time they led to the famous series of half-track gun tractors used extensively by the Germans in all theatres of the Second World War. They fall outside the armoured half-track story except for a few late-war extemporised conversions. However, the half-tracks in the 1-tonne and 3-tonne classes were developed further into armoured vehicles as well, and the two types formed the basis for the standardised infantry carriers which equipped the Panzer Grenadiers in many forms in the Second World War.

It was in 1935 that the idea of adapting the new artillery tractors took root. By this time the plans for the new Panzer Divisions were well in hand and the first tanks (PzKpfw I and II) were in production. To carry a complete infantry section or squad of ten men the 3-tonne tractor chassis was of suitable size. The choice of this chassis may also have been influenced by the construction by Rheinmetall in 1935 of an experimental armoured self-propelled anti-tank gun, the 37-mm *Selbstfahrlafette* L/70, which had a 37-mm anti-tank gun in a fully traversing turret. It was tested by *Heereswaffenamt*, but never put into production.

The armoured troop carrier version was started in 1937 and only minimal changes were needed – such as canting back the steering wheel – to suit the basic chassis to the armoured superstructure's shape. A faceted, well-sloped armoured body was designed with a strong family resemblance to that used on the armoured cars. Development vehicles included some with rear engines, but it was decided that simple open bodies allowing troops to disembark from the back doors or over the sides were more practical, so the armoured personnel carriers retained the same front engined layout as the artillery tractors. The prototype, designated *Gepanzerter Mannschrafts-transportwagen* (Gp MTW) was ready in 1938 and was rushed into production after

SdKfz 251/9
Medium Half-track with 75-mm Gun
Length: 19·02 ft *Width:* 6·89 ft *Weight:* 18,800
lb *Speed:* 34 mph *Range:* 185 miles *Armour:* 12
mm max *Armament:* 75-mm StuK 37; 1×7·92-
mm MG 42 (some models only)

successful trials. At that time the Panzer
Divisions' motorised infantry was still
lorry-borne and there was an urgent need
to give them armoured vehicles. The current
(1938) production version of the 3-tonne
tractor was used, the H kl 6, and this basic
design was 'frozen' and used until 1945,
though many details on the vehicle were
changed as time went by.

The Hanomag-built chassis had a body
by Büssing-NAG. There was a frontal
armour of 14·5 mm, with 8 mm on the sides.
The vehicle was given the ordnance designation SdKfz 251, the appellation by which it
is best known, and was called the *Mittlerer
Schutzenpanzerwagen* (medium infantry
armoured vehicle). The first production
vehicles were ready in the spring of 1939
and went to equip an infantry company in I
Panzer Division for troop trials. General
Heinz Guderian, Inspector General of
Armoured Troops, among others, was highly
impressed and called for further developments to make the vehicle of universal use
within the armoured division.

By the time the Germans invaded Poland
in September 1939 more SdKfz 251s were in
service (now also with II Panzer Division)
and they spearheaded the attack along with
the tanks. This was the first full-scale
vindication of the ideas first put forward by
Liddell Hart and other protagonists of
armoured warfare.

To a great extent the SdKfz 251 was a
compromise. It was not as heavily armoured
as might have been desired and it was in
essence no more than an armoured taxi, for
the idea then was simply that the infantry
should be carried in the protected vehicle
where they would de-bus to fight on foot.
However, for its period, it was revolutionary,
and directly spurred on the Americans to
develop their own similar armoured half-
track, the M3.

*In an SdKfz 251/6, Luftwaffe officers co-ordinate
an attack while a panzer commander looks on*

While other nations' half-tracks mostly
used the simple rubber band and spring
bogie half-track unit of the type produced
by Kégresse and his imitators, the German
half-tracks were radically different and
highly sophisticated for the period.

Strictly speaking the chassis was a three-
quarter track: normal front wheels, steered
conventionally, supported the front end and
the actual drive was taken via the transmission to the front sprocket wheels of the long
track units. These supported the weight of
the vehicle, and a Cletrac-type steering unit
(a controlled differential transmission with
steering brakes on the shaft) was fitted
within the drive system on the front axle
of the suspension. The sprocket wheels had
rollers on the wheel perimeter rather than
actual sprocket teeth to engage the track.

The Cletrac steering unit acted as the
front wheel was steered, thus braking the
tracks as required to assist the vehicle
round the radius of the turn; brake drums
were an integral part of the drive wheels.
The tracks themselves were of highly
sophisticated design, with sealed, lubricated
needle roller bearings on the track pins, and
detachable rubber track pads on the inside
to cushion the wheel paths and engage the
sprocket rollers positively. These features
gave long track life and excellent traction,
but they were of high quality and thus
expensive to produce. Later production
vehicles had sprocket teeth of conventional
type and dry pin tracks to simplify production and reduce costs. The suspension was
by sprung torsion bars and the wheels were
interleaved and of the perforated disc type
with solid rubber tyres. The interleaved
suspension was designed to give excellent
flotation, though as with all other examples
of this German interleaved suspension they
were vulnerable to frozen snow if parked
overnight.

The gearbox was a four-speed type with two-speed auxiliary boxes for cross-country driving. There were eight forward and two reverse gears. Steering was of the Ackermann type and the controlled differential steering came into operation automatically after the front wheels were turned more than a certain amount. The hand brake and foot brake both operated on the track brakes.

The chassis was of conventional girder frame type of welded girder construction with cross-members. There were armoured belly plates under the chassis and the hull itself was in two sections bolted together, the front one consisting of the engine and driving compartments, the other containing the passenger and fighting compartment. In most cases the hull was of welded construction, but there was an alternative riveted body since some firms in the SdKfz 251 construction group had facilities for riveting but not for welding. The SdKfz 251 became a major production type and by 1944 nearly 16,000 had been built by a consortium of companies which included Skoda, Adler, and Auto-Union with many small sub-contractors. Production figures of 348 in 1940 increased to 7800 by 1944. The engine was a Maybach HL 42 6-cylinder, 100-hp water-cooled unit of 4 litres.

Simplifying production

There were four basic production models, each a further simplification of its predecessor with a view to reducing production time and costs. Mechanically they were all similar but there were external detail differences. Ausf A, which was the first production type in 1939, had three prominent vision ports in each side of the superstructure. The radio aerial was fitted on the right front fender and a simple swivel bracket without a shield of any kind was provided at the front and rear ends of the fighting compartment. The Ausf A was soon succeeded by the Ausf B (the major type in service in 1940) which incorporated all the improvements suggested by early experience. The side vision ports were omitted, leaving only those in the front superstructure for the driver and commander. Tools and equipment were re-arranged and the characteristic shield for the forward MG 34 mount was added. Stowage lockers were fitted each side between the mudguards and the superstructure.

The Ausf C went into production in mid-1940, though production of the Ausf B continued until the end of that year. The Ausf C again featured all the improvements resulting from further battle experience. A single front plate was fitted on the nose, replacing an angled two-piece plate on earlier models. The radiator was now exposed to the bottom of the vehicle but armoured cooling intakes were fitted prominently on the sides of the engine compartment (some late Ausf Bs also had these). The radio aerial was resited on the superstructure in both the Ausf B and C.

By 1942 the German economy was suffering from the war effort, and losses on the Russian Front were making swift replacement of material imperative. To speed up production and cut costs many sorts of German AFV were simplified as far as possible. In the case of the SdKfz 251 this involved greatly simplifying the armoured superstructure to eliminate all unnecessary machining and fabrication time. Faceted areas, such as at the back and the engine compartment sides, were replaced by single large plates. The engine air intakes were abandoned and the stowage boxes at the sides, originally detachable, were built in as part of the structure, while the vision ports were replaced by simple vision slits. The all-welded Ausf D was in production up to the end of the war.

The basic vehicle had a simple interior with padded bench seats along each side to hold nine or ten men. The complete infantry squad with their MG 34 rode the vehicle, four vehicles carrying a complete infantry platoon and ten vehicles carrying a complete company – with the company commander riding in the tenth vehicle. In fact there was a lot of variety in actual establishment due to the fact that supply could never keep up with demand. In theory, all four battalions of a Panzer Grenadier Brigade would be wholly equipped with half-tracks but in reality only one battalion, or at best two, would have them, the remaining battalions being equipped only with trucks. Thus the half-tracks tended to go to the best battalions, and elite divisions like Panzer Division Gross-Deutschland or Waffen-SS Panzer divisions would generally have the most generous allocations.

Within a Panzer Division the task of an armoured battalion of Panzer Grenadiers was to follow closely on the heels of the attacking tanks, co-operating with them as the situation demanded. The usual German method of tank attack was to concentrate first on any enemy artillery with the first wave of tanks and either eliminate the enemy, force them to withdraw, or throw them into chaos. The second wave was usually accompanied by the Panzer Grenadiers in their half-tracks and the task of this wave was to engage enemy infantry and anti-tank guns. Assault guns were also generally employed at this stage, possibly substituting for the second wave of tanks. A third wave of tanks or assault guns with an accompanying wave of Panzer Grenadiers would concentrate on mopping up or engaging any remaining pockets of resistance. The motorised infantry battalion carried in ordinary trucks (the second battalion of the regiment) would then relieve the armoured battalion, so that the armoured element was freed if necessary to carry on the forward push. This, at least, was the theory, and while there were textbook attacks carried out this way there were many variations on the theme.

For example, in an attack on a major target, dive-bombing by Stukas or a big artillery bombardment would be carried out rapidly and with great precision. Tanks and Panzer Grenadiers would encircle the target area while the bombardment took place, then half the force would turn inwards to make an attack from the rear, while the other half maintained the circle, partly to stave off any attempted counter-attack but also to catch any enemy forces attempting to flee the area.

Panzer Grenadiers were also used as an actual spearhead attack force in some cases where the defending forces were only lightly equipped. Here tanks engaged the enemy forces with the maximum amount of noise or fire, then drew the enemy fire while a Panzer Grenadier company in half-tracks made a swift flank attack from another direction. This was a favourite tactic for capturing defended points and bridges. In defence, a typical tactic was the reverse of this. The Panzer Grenadiers would engage the enemy frontally while tanks attempted to work their way round to attack the flanks.

The need for Panzer Grenadiers to spearhead their own attacks led to the development of many of the variants of the SdKfz 251, for the armed versions which appeared gave further strength to their own fire-power. In effect the family of SdKfz 251 variants gave the Panzer Grenadiers their own range of armed vehicles to back up the requirements of the armoured infantry. There were 23 official variants, most of them used in armoured divisions, and there were also unofficial variations.

One variation of the basic vehicle, SdKfz 251/1, carried a quadrant and mount for the 'heavy' MG 34 machine-gun, ie, on its adjustable tripod mount with optical sight. There was no armoured shield and a second MG 34 with heavy mount was carried in the vehicle. This variation was used by the heavy machine-gun squads of the heavy or support platoons. The standard SdKfz 251/1 carried MG 34s in their 'light' form only.

One of the most spectacular variations of this vehicle was also designated SdKfz 251/1 but it was fitted with six frames for launching 280-mm or 320-mm *Wurfkorper* rockets. Three launching frames were carried on each side, and the rockets had jellied petrol warheads. Basically the idea was to provide heavy fire support cheaply, using existing types of rocket. The frames were attached at about 45° elevation and the entire vehicle was lined up for firing. There was a sight vane on the engine cover for the driver's use, but sometimes the commander used an artillery type periscope for more accurate sighting. The rockets – also known as *Wurfrahmen* – were fired in succession, not together. The whole set-up was crude, but proved quite effective, specially in street fighting. In Stalingrad and Warsaw these weapons were used with spectacular and terrifying results. They were easy to load and made the vehicle into a useful type of terror weapon.

Mortar carrier

Just as the SdKfz 251/1 served the needs of the rifle squads, so the vehicle was adapted to carry the 80-mm mortar of the heavy support company. It could be fired from the vehicle if necessary, but was normally fired from cover on the ground. Some of the seating was taken out of this variant to allow stowage space for the mortar ammunition. Later in the war the light half-track, SdKfz 250, was more commonly used as a mortar carrier, since the SdKfz 251 was larger than was really necessary and half-tracks were in short supply.

For unit commanders, the SdKfz 251/3 was equipped with a medium-wave radio set, for maintaining regimental and divisional links, fitted with the characteristic bedstead aerial. The vehicle took over the functions of the radio-equipped armoured cars in the early years of the war. After about 1942 a sectional aerial mast replaced the bedstead aerial. A second version of the 251/3 was fitted with extra radio equipment for communicating with tanks when operating with tank and other AFV formations. Later models had pole aerials in the usual style and differed little externally from the standard model. Yet further variations of the SdKfz 251/3 were built for other special communications roles, some for large formation command use and others for air control and liaison.

The SdKfz 251/4 was a special infantry gun tractor for hauling the 105-mm guns in

SdKfz 251/16
Medium Half-track with Flame-thrower

Length: 19·03 ft *Width:* 6·89 ft *Weight:* 19,180 lb *Speed:* 34 mph *Range:* 185 miles *Armour:* 12 mm max *Armament:* 2 x 14-mm flame projectors; 1 x 7·92-mm MG 34

An SdKfz 251/1 follows an Sdkfz 251/10 (with 37-mm gun) across a frozen Russian landscape

armoured divisions. It was also used to tow other types of gun such as the 50-mm Pak 38, the 75-mm Pak 40, and the 105-mm *Leichte Feldhaubitze* 18, among others. Externally the vehicle resembled the SdKfz 251/1 but without the machine-gun mounts.

The SdKfz 251/5 was yet another variant for carrying the various assault engineers of an armoured battalion with their inflatable boats and assault bridges. Another variant – the *Pioneerpanzerwagen* – was the SdKfz 251/7 which had special fittings

on the superstructure sides to carry assault bridge ramps. Assault boats and demolition stores were carried.

The SdKfz 251/6 was an important command version elaborately equipped for the use of senior formation commanders. It had comprehensive office facilities with map-boards, cypher and encoding machines, and multi-wave radio equipment in a variety of alternative combinations. The vehicle was popularly known as a *Kommandopanzer-wagen* and was used by virtually all Army,

Army Group, and Divisional commanders.

The SdKfz 251/8 was an armoured ambulance – *Krankenpanzerwagen* – with racks for two stretchers. It could carry two litters and four seated wounded, or the stretcher racks could be folded back to provide for eight seated wounded. This variant carried no armament.

The first half-track to have a gun fitted was the SdKfz 251/10 which was given a 37-mm Pak 36 mounted on the forward superstructure. The idea was postulated as early as the original troop trials using the vehicle in 1939, and by 1940 the first SdKfz 251/10s were in service. The Pak 36 was simply the complete weapon less its wheels and field carriage. The platoon leader's vehicle was usually an SdKfz 251/10 and its function was to provide covering fire for the other vehicles of the platoon.

In later vehicles the original high gun shield was considerably reduced, and some had no shield at all or a shield on one side only. These were common variations of the half-track. The second gun-armed variant to be produced in quantity was the SdKfz 251/9 which entered service in 1942. It carried the familiar 75-mm KwK 37 L/24 short low velocity gun of the type originally carried by the PzKpfw IV.

When the Panzer IV began to be equipped with the long 75-mm gun there was a gap in the armoury of an armoured division in that the usefulness of the short gun as a support weapon was missed. Assault guns filled this gap to some extent, but they were not always available. Moreover, it was useful for the Panzer Grenadiers to have their own fire support capacity, and most battalions had a gun company of six of these vehicles. The L/24 gun was mounted above the front of the superstructure. Later conversions had raised armour plates on the sides to protect the crew. This was a popular and valuable vehicle known to the men as *Stummel* (Stump). The SdKfz 251/11 was a telephone line layer, equipped with cables and apparatus for rigging field telephones. SdKfz 251/12, 251/13, 251/14 and 251/15 were all specialist artillery vehicles for such functions as artillery survey, sound ranging, and flash spotting. They were used by assault gun units and artillery units within the armoured division.

Flame-throwing half-track

An interesting and potent variant was SdKfz 215/16, the *Flammpanzerwagen* which carried two 700-litre flame-fuel tanks and two 14-mm projectors, one on each side of the superstructure. Some models had a third projector on a long hose extension for use outside the vehicle. The rear doors were welded shut as the flame fuel tanks were in the hull rear. Up to 80 two-second bursts of flame were possible with the equipment and the range was up to 35 metres.

SdKfz 251/17 was another type introduced in 1942, with a 20-mm Flak 30 or Flak 38 mounted in the rear compartment. There were several variations in the mounting, and those with the Flak 38 sometimes had bulged superstructure sides that let down to give better traverse and more room for the crew in action. These vehicles were intended to give anti-aircraft support for Panzer and Panzer Grenadier units, but the guns could be (and often were) used against ground targets.

Also designated SdKfz 251/17 was an elaborate design with enclosed remote-control turret which entered service in very small numbers in 1944. There was a covered front end where the small turret was located. Armament consisted of the Flak 38 20-mm gun.

SdKfz 251/18 was an armoured observation vehicle for artillery use, and 251/19 was a telephone exchange vehicle used by communications units. Of greater interest was SdKfz 251/20 *Uhu* (owl) which gave the Army 'eyes' for night fighting. Developed in 1944, when special night attack units were formed, each with six Panther tanks, it carried an infrared searchlight (*Beobachtungs Gerät* 251) on a turntable mount in the rear compartment. A special sighting telescope was also carried in the vehicle. In action the searchlight operator picked out suitable targets with the searchlight beam – which was of course invisible to the human eye – then called up the Panther tank to engage the target. The tank also had its own, less powerful, night sights, and could spot targets unaided by *Uhu* at up to 500 metres. This was the start of what is now a standard aspect of armoured warfare – night fighting – and almost all modern AFVs carry infrared searchlights.

Allied air superiority was a constant problem for ground forces by 1944, and one

expedient produced at this time was SdKfz 251/21, a *Flakpanzerwagen* fitted with three 15-mm Drilling MG 151 machine-guns in a triple shielded mount. The guns were obsolete Luftwaffe pieces and the conversion added a cheap but effective Flak vehicle to the inventory.

More firepower against the ever-growing number of tanks led to the 1944 conversion of the SdKfz 251/22 which originated as a last ditch SP vehicle exactly like the SdKfz 234/4 armoured car. Hitler ordered

maximum self-propelled anti-tank firepower and the Pak 40 75-mm gun was simply fitted into the fighting compartment of the half-track, just as in the armoured car. The wheels and trails were removed and the roof of the driving compartment was cut out to facilitate gun traverse. Like the SdKfz 234/4, this was a most effective expedient, and although the 251/22 was not as mobile, it was built in larger numbers.

This was the last official version of the ubiquitous 3-tonne half-track, though there

were numerous prototypes carrying such pieces as 88-mm Pak guns, *Flakvierling* quad 20-mm mounts, and a variety of old tank turrets and odd weapons. It had proved to be a remarkable and immortal vehicle, and the Skoda-built model of the SdKfz 251 emerged again after the Second World War. Basically similar to the Ausf D version of the original design, it was designated OT-810 and remained as one of the standard troop carriers of the Czechoslovakian Army well into the 1970s.

LIGHT HALF-TRACKS

Second only to the 3-tonne armoured half-track in importance was the 1-tonne model or *Leichter Schutzenpanzerwagen* which complemented the heavier vehicle and, in some forms, took over the functions of armoured cars. The original 1-tonne unarmoured half-track appeared with the other series of prototype machines in 1934–35, built in this case by Demag.

It was intended at the time specifically for infantry roles such as towing the small 37-mm anti-tank gun, the 75-mm infantry howitzer, or ammunition trailers. With a simple truck-like engine cover and an open body it was taken into service as the SdKfz 10 *Leichter Zugkraftwagen* (light prime mover). Pre-production models culminated in the definitive Demag D7 of 1939, which became the major service version and remained in production until 1944. Mechanically this was a most efficient little vehicle, and as with the Hanomag, there was a big group of contractors and subcontractors involved in production work.

By 1939, when the prototype Hanomag 3-tonne half-track SdKfz 251 had proved successful, the Army's thoughts turned to utilising the 1-tonne half-track in a similar fashion by giving it an armoured body. The only snag was that the vehicle was very small (15·3 ft long, 6 ft high, and 5·75 ft wide) and of limited power, having a Maybach HL 42 100 hp engine. With the added weight of an armoured body, it was feared that performance would be reduced, but this problem was overcome by shortening the suspension so that the vehicle had one less road wheel on each side.

Büssing-NAG accordingly designed a scaled down version of the armoured body used on the 3-tonne vehicle and fitted it to a prototype shortened chassis supplied to them by Demag. The resulting prototype performed well and the type was ordered into instant production. It was not so successful as the 3-tonne model, carrying only six men and having inferior performance. However, in certain functions it proved itself. It was ideal as a platoon or company commander's vehicle, as an 80-mm mortar carrier, and as an observation vehicle. Where it could do the same job as a 3-tonne and thus release the 3-tonne for more urgent functions, the small half-track was a valuable asset.

In its armoured form the 1-tonne vehicle was designated SdKfz 250 *Leichter Schutzenpanzerwagen.* Some 14 variants were produced, several of them parallel in function to the SdKfz 251 variants, and in this respect the vehicles were interchangeable. The basic SdKfz 250 was 15 ft long, 6·2 ft wide, and 6·4 ft high. Its top speed was 37 mph and the Maybach Variorex gearbox gave a choice of seven forward and three reverse gears. Mechanically the SdKfz 250 was similar to the SdKfz 251; wheels, suspension and track arrangements were all basically the same except in physical disposition. The combat weight of the vehicle was 5·3 tons (1 tonne was the payload) and the armour was 14·5 mm thick at the front and 8 mm elsewhere. The early vehicles entered service in 1940 and were

first used in the invasion of France. Production continued until 1943 in the vehicle's original form, after which the body was slightly simplified (as with the 3-tonne vehicles) to expedite production.

Because of its small size, stowage arrangements in the SdKfz 250 were very compact. The original superstructure was quite complicated in shape, being 'bowed' outward in the middle to give maximum passenger space. Like that of the 3-tonner, the body was faceted with multi-angled plates. The modifications made in 1943 were considerable: the number of panels used in constructing the body was reduced by nearly half; integral side stowage lockers were built in; front and rear plates were reduced to single pieces; vision flaps were replaced by slits; a larger rear door was fitted; hoops were fitted to support a canvas cover over the passenger compartment; and headlights were eliminated in favour of a standard *Notek* night driving light.

The basic model, essentially a plain armoured troop carrier, was designated SdKfz 250/1 and was principally used by platoon and company commanders. Like the 3-tonne model it normally had two MG 34s on pivot mounts, but sometimes had only one, or carried the heavy tripod-mounted version. Apart from the basic radio-telephone set the vehicle could carry another set if necessary for a particular command function.

Communications equipment

The second model produced was the SdKfz 250/2 telephone line layer which was also used as an observation vehicle. Carrier frames for field telephone lines were supplied and could be fitted on the mudguards or in the fighting compartment. Up to three cables could be laid at a time. A radio set (*Funksprechgerät F,* the R/T set in all vehicles) was standard equipment (in the front superstructure ahead of the passenger seat alongside the driver) throughout the SdKfz 250 series.

The Sdkfz 250/3 was the *Leichter Funkpanzerwagen* and like other radio vehicles had the inevitable bedstead frame aerial. As with the 3-tonne equivalent, several sub-variants of this vehicle had different radio equipment according to their function, although externally they were all similar. One of the most famous wartime vehicles was of this type – Rommel's personal command and liaison vehicle, *Greif,* which he used while commanding the Afrika Korps in the Western Desert in 1942. Later examples of the SdKfz 250/3 had the bedstead aerials replaced by pole and star aerials as required and externally were similar to the basic SdKfz 250/1 when their aerials were dismantled.

The SdKfz 250/4, an air liaison or observation post vehicle, was specifically intended to carry the staff of assault gun batteries. A 1943 production vehicle on the simplified chassis, it replaced an earlier type, the SdKfz 253. The SdKfz 250/5 *Leichter Beobachtungspanzerwagen* was a similar vehicle intended for the same role. Externally it resembled the SdKfz 250/1, but it

had the necessary radio equipment for its observation post role.

Next in the series, SdKfz 250/6, was a specialised ammunition carrier for assault guns. There were two variations, one with racks for 70 rounds for the short 75-mm gun and another which carried 60 rounds for the long 75-mm gun.

SdKfz 250/7 was a specialist 80-mm mortar carrier, which largely replaced the 3-tonner in this role. Another version of the 250/7 had racks for carrying 80-mm mortar ammunition, and was often used to transport the commander of the heavy platoon of a Panzer Grenadier battalion. The mortar of an SdKfz 250/7 could be fired from the vehicle but was fired from the ground whenever possible.

A 1-tonne version of the 3-tonne half-track with 75-mm short gun was an obvious development, and the SdKfz 250/8 came into service in 1943 to equip the heavy gun platoon of a Panzer Grenadier battalion, (with six vehicles to a platoon). In all respects, it was similar to the 3-tonne vehicle. An MG 42 was mounted above the gun to act as a ranging piece and to give local defence fire.

By 1942 the armoured car had been proved unsuitable for the Russian Front, and half-tracks had a better survival and maintenance record than wheeled vehicles. In severe snow and mud the four wheeled armoured cars were very limited in operation. It was therefore decided to replace armoured cars as far as possible by half-tracks. This decision resulted in the SdKfz 250/9 *Leichter Schutzenpanzerwagen* (20-mm) being built to replace the SdKfz 222 armoured cars. The SdKfz 250/9 simply had the complete turret assembly of the SdKfz 222 armoured car placed atop the superstructure, which was suitably roofed in. In effect a half-track armoured car was the result. The six-sided turret retained the mesh anti-grenade covers. Later vehicles had a simpler turret.

Further self-propelled gun vehicles were also produced. Just as the 37-mm Pak gun was fitted to the SdKfz 251 half-track (resulting in the SdKfz 251/10 platoon commander's vehicle), an identical operation converted the 1-tonne vehicle to the SdKfz 250/10. This was the first gun-armed variant to appear in service, during the 1940 campaigns. A similar vehicle, the SdKfz 250/11, replaced the SdKfz 250/10 from 1942. This had the tapered bore 20-mm *Schwerer Panzerbusche* 41 mounted on the superstructure front.

The remaining variants of the 1-tonne half-track were all ancillary vehicles for artillery use. SdKfz 250/12 was a *Leichter Messtruppanzerwagen* (light artillery survey vehicle) which was equipped with range-finding periscopes and levelling and signalling apparatus for the control of artillery batteries.

A very early variant of the SdKfz 250 was a light ammunition carrier designed specifically to support the new family of assault guns. It had a different ordnance inventory number, SdKfz 252, and was a good example of the thoroughness with which the Panzer

*Into action on the Russian Front: Panzer Gren-
adiers leap from their half-track*

Divisions were planned. Purpose-built for its single support role, its body was distinctively cut away to keep weight to a minimum. It was fully enclosed, with hatches for the crew members and double doors at the rear to give access to the ammunition compartment. A two-wheel trailer carrying additional ammunition was towed.

During the invasion of France SdKfz 252s acted as limber vehicles for the new StuG IIIs, but it was quickly realised that such a purpose-built vehicle was a luxury, even in 1940, and production soon ceased. Thereafter the basic vehicle was adapted for use as a munitions carrier and redesigned SdKfz 250/6 as previously described.

Also dating from the early period was the SdKfz 253 *Leichter Gepanzerter Beobachtungskraftwagen* (light armoured observation vehicle), another fully enclosed type which was intended as a command vehicle for the assault gun batteries. As with the munition carrier, however, it proved an elaborate luxury and was an early victim of rationalisation. Subsequently the basic SdKfz 250 vehicle was adapted for the observation post role as the 250/4 and 250/5.

As these early changes indicate, it was apparent almost from the first that having armoured half-tracks in both the 1-tonne and 3-tonne classes was not altogether satisfactory. There was much duplication of production effort, only a limited number of common components for maintenance purposes, while the 1-tonne vehicle was too small for some roles (eg troop carrying) and the 3-tonner was over-large for some of its roles (eg mortar carrying). This conclusion led to an attempt to rationalise the armoured half-track into one single design.

Stemming directly from the existing vehicles, the HK 600 series of prototypes were built by Demag and Hanomag in 1942, with a strong family resemblance to the SdKfz 251 half-track. The old division into 1-tonne and 3-tonne classes was retained, the HKp 606 being a 1-tonner and the HKp 603 a 3-tonner. They were greatly simplified in comparison with the SdKfz 250 and 251, in order to reduce costs and production time. They were not so radically improved, however, as to justify disrupting production of the SdKfz 250 and 251 at a time when these vehicles were needed more urgently than ever. Consequently, the HK 600 prototypes were abandoned in 1943, but the work was not wasted: many of the simplified features of the superstructures were used in the 1943 rationalisation programmes of the SdKfz 250 and 251.

Hitler's promptings led *Heereswaffenamt* to seek an altogether more radical solution. While some of Hitler's ideas proved wildly impractical or fanciful, many of his fundamental notions were proved right. Indeed, in his desire to standardise effort where possible, and to go for maximum armour and firepower, he was usually some way ahead of his AFV advisers.

In May 1942, he suggested the development of new 'locust-like' vehicles to overcome all the difficulties of traction encountered during the first severe winter on the Russian Front. They were to be both simple and easily adaptable to all functions. Hitler wanted them to be in production within a year and the Adler firm was given the task of making two prototypes. These were ready at the end of 1942 and were known as LeWS (*Leichter Wehrmachtschlepper* or light military tractor).

The LeWS was radically different from

Rommel's personal command car, Greif, *an SdKfz 250/3 light armoured half-track*

SdKfz 250/5
Light Half-track with Radio

the SdKfz 250 and emphasised the passing of the leisurely days of complicated automotive engineering. The LeWS had a simple chassis, pressed steel disc road wheels, low pressure front tyres, steel dry pin semi-tracks, and used tank type sprockets and idlers. The armoured front cab and engine compartment followed the layout of a conventional truck and the engine was an ordinary Maybach HL 30 four-cylinder unit, restricting maximum speed to only 17 mph. The body floor took the form of a flat pan so that various ordnance mountings or self-contained superstructures could be simply bolted on. All fabrication was of flat plates and simple pressings. Provision was made for production without the cab so that a completely integral cab and superstructure could be fitted to certain versions.

However, the promising LeWS was never proceeded with, probably because it still did not overcome the problem of two different weight classes. In any case, a full-tracked truck, the *Raupenschlepper Ost* (tracked tractor Eastfront) was being produced to meet many of the same requirements. It was even cheaper and simpler to build so that production of LeWS would have involved precisely the sort of duplication the design had set out to avoid. A third LeWS prototype was built in 1944 and there were plans for a fourth with Maybach-Olvar tank type transmission, but the *Leichter Wehrmachtschlepper* was a lost cause and was never ordered.

A companion design, however, the *Schwerer Wehrmachtschlepper* (SWS – heavy military tractor), had a more successful history and was the nearest the Wehrmacht came to a standardised half-track replacement for the earlier designs. It was actually intended to replace the 5-tonne (unarmoured) series of artillery tractor half-tracks and was produced with a cargo body and unarmoured truck type front end for this role. Like the LeWS, the SWS was produced with an armoured cab and engine cover, and a flat body floor to which various combinations of ordnance and superstructure could be fitted. The prototype was built in 1942, and although production did not start until late 1943, the type saw wide and useful service in the last 18 months of the war.

The basic vehicle was produced as an armoured supply truck or munitions carrier with plain wire-mesh drop sides. The most important variants, however, were those fitted with the 150-mm *Panzerwerfer* 42 rocket launcher and the 37-mm Flak43 AA gun. The former had a low armoured superstructure in which the rounds were carried with the ten-barrel launcher in a traversing mount on top of the superstructure. The Flak gun version retained the wire mesh drop sides of the supply carrier with the traversing gun mount welded to the body floor.

Captured half-tracks

The SWS was the final development of the German armoured half-tracks, but in addition to their own vehicles, the conquests of 1939–41 brought them a number of foreign half-tracks which were added to the stock of German built vehicles.

France was the major European builder of half-tracks before the war and the Unic – and Somua-Kégresse were the standard French types. The Somua was the most widely used, and fitting armoured bodies to it produced an armoured personnel carrier similar to the SdKfz 251. This

SdKfz 250/7
Light Half-track with 80-mm Mortar

SdKfz 250/8
Light Half-track with 75-mm Gun
Length· 14·96 ft *Width:* 6·4 ft *Weight:*
12,565 lb *Speed:* 40 mph *Range:* 200 miles
Armour: 12 mm max *Armament:* 75-mm KwK 37;
1 x 7·92-mm MG 34

*September 1941: German troops with their SdKfz
253 light observation vehicle watch smoke rising
from the city of Novgorod, set on fire by the retreating Russian troops*

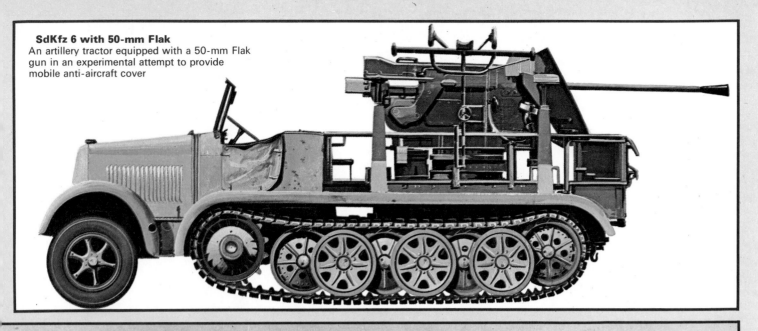

SdKfz 6 with 50-mm Flak
An artillery tractor equipped with a 50-mm Flak gun in an experimental attempt to provide mobile anti-aircraft cover

Associated Press

vehicle was designated *Mittlerer Schutz-enpanzerwagen* S 307 (f) and was used as a troop carrier and 105-mm howitzer tractor in some armoured divisions. A further armoured conversion was built in occupied France and consisted of 16 captured French 80-mm mortars mounted on a traversing mount in a twin bank on the rear chassis. Another variant carried a 150-mm *Panzer-werfer* 42 launcher (mounted as in the SWS), while a 1944 conversion mounted the 75-mm Pak 40.

The Unic-Kégresse half-track was also given an armoured superstructure. Designated *Leichter Schutzenpanzerwagen* U 304 (f), it was used as a substitute for the SdKfz 250 by German units based in France.

Conscripted vehicles

As the war situation deteriorated, all sorts of vehicles not intended for offensive use were given armoured bodywork and pressed into service with first line units. An early example was the experimental fitting of a captured Russian 76·2-mm anti-tank gun to an SdKfz 6 5-ton half-track tractor. Only nine such vehicles (popularly known as Diana) were converted and some were sent to Libya in 1942. This opened up the idea of further conversion and many un-armoured half-tracks were given armoured cabs and superstructures.

This was particularly true of vehicles with anti-aircraft mounts. Allied air superiority on all fronts meant the Germans had to divert a lot of resources into providing air defence for their ground troops – unlike the Allies, who were much less frequently bothered by the Luftwaffe.

Some SdKfz 9 18-ton half-tracks – the largest of all – were given armoured cabs and engine covers and fitted with the 88-mm Flak 37 gun. The SdKfz 7/1, SdKfz 10/5 and SdKfz 7/2 all had anti-aircraft mounts and varying degrees of improvised armour protection.

Finally, there was the Maultier truck, a 3-tonne capacity lorry converted to a half-track. Initially the idea stemmed from a field conversion in Russia, where some troops placed Panzer I track units on a truck in place of the rear wheels. Subsequently Fords, Opels and Daimlers were given factory conversions to compensate for the lateness of the *Schwerer Wehrmachtschlepper*. Even some 4·5-tonne Mercedes trucks were converted with PzKpfw II track units. The Opel model was the most numerous of these, and to help overcome the constant shortage of armoured half-tracks it was decided to design an armoured superstructure for it. Some 3000 armoured versions of the Opel Maultier were ordered and delivered in 1944–45 as armoured gun tractors/munition carriers. They were used for towing wheeled *Nebel-werfer* mounts, with the rockets carried in the armoured body.

A further 300 Maultiers were ordered to be fitted with the 150-mm *Panzerwerfer* 42. The ten-barrel launcher was fitted on a low superstructure as in the SWS, and the Maultier and SWS were used interchange-ably as the standard mobile rocket launcher for specialist rocket troop regiments in armoured divisions. Again, it must be stressed that this was an expedient design – no more than a lightly armoured tracked lorry – but it was quite an effective design.

The last half-track worthy of mention was not an armoured vehicle at all – the tiny NSU *Kettenrad*, a half-track motor-cycle. Produced as part of the Wehrmacht's half-track series, it was designated HK 100. The front forks and suspension were of motorcycle type and the rear end was made up of a punt type chassis with miniature half-tracks. The engine was a water-cooled 1·5 litre Opel motor car unit of 36 hp. Top speed was 50 mph.

The original idea was to provide a small tractor for the use of airborne troops, and the design work was conditioned by the need for a vehicle light enough and small enough to be carried by the standard Junkers Ju 52 transport. The *Kettenrad* could be slung between the aircraft's undercarriage or manhandled (just) through the fuselage cargo door. It could tow a light ammunition trailer, a 28-mm or 37-mm anti-tank gun, or a 75-mm light infantry gun. It was designated SdKfz 2 *Kleine Kettenrad*. The first examples were issued for service in June 1941 and the type became immensely popular with the troops specially on the Russian Front. A couple of variants carried reels or spools in the rear compartment for telephone or cable laying. An enlarged version, the *Grosse Kettenrad*, was projected but resources were not available for such luxuries and it never went into production.

End of the line

The half-track had almost had its day by 1945. It was complicated to build and a compromise in performance terms. The open top, while considered satisfactory in the late 1930s, left much to be desired when the occupants came up against aircraft straf-ing and shell splinters.

This is not to say that armoured half-tracks were not valuable. The Panzer Divisions with their combination of tanks and half-tracks and the tactics that went with them were almost unbeatable until they were overwhelmed by sheer weight of numbers. By 1942 there were sufficient half-tracks available for all Panzer Divisions to have one or more battalions of Panzer Grenadiers equipped with half-tracks and over 15,000 of the 3-tonne model alone were built. Increased firepower was provided by adding the self-propelled gun variants to the armoured infantry battalions, but the grave shortage of vehicles was inevitably revealed.

A replacement vehicle for the armoured half-track was planned, to apply all the les-sons of five years of war. It was intended to base a new fully-tracked armoured troop carrier on the chassis of the small but highly efficient Czech PzKpfw 38(t), and to use the German adaptation of the chassis as the basis for a whole series of vehicles.

The armoured personnel carrier variant, *Schutzenpanzerwagen* Ausf 38(t), would have been fully enclosed and would have had rear doors and a 20-mm gun in a traversing turret. However, by the closing months of the war there was little chance of the project proceeding beyond the drawing board stage and no prototype ever materi-alised. While no new half-track designs have appeared since the German and American types of the Second World War, virtually all tracked armoured personnel carriers built by the major powers since then have been of the full-track type similar to that planned by the Wehrmacht in 1945.

Panzerwerfer 42 ten-barrel 150-mm rocket launcher mounted on the back of a converted Opel Maultier truck. More than 3000 of these trucks were con-verted to half-tracks, 300 of them with the Panzer-werfer *mountings*

Opel Maultier Panzerwerfer Half-track
Conversion

THE FIRST PANZERS
THE LESSONS OF DEFEAT

Tanks were instrumental in the final defeat of the German Imperial Army. Forbidden heavy weapons by the Treaty of Versailles, a group of young German officers were already planning a new kind of warfare. The cardboard chariots of the *Reichswehr* became the hard steel of Nazi Germany's first Panzer Divisions

The story of the German panzers really starts in 1926, well before the rise of the National Socialist party as a major force in Germany, and about ten years before the massive 'Guns before Butter' re-armament of Germany under the Nazi regime gained real momentum in 1936. Back in 1926 the German armed forces were still very much affected by the savage restrictions of the Treaty of Versailles, signed in 1919 after the First World War. Among the conditions of the treaty were a limitation of the army to 100,000 men without tanks of any kind, and an allowance of a small number of armoured cars solely for border patrol work.

General von Seeckt, C-in-C of the *Reichswehr* (German Army) until 1926, was a far-sighted man who had learned the

lessons of the First World War – that mobility and flexibility, as demonstrated by the early British tanks in 1917/18, pointed the way to the warfare of the future. Within the limitations imposed on him, von Seeckt made good use of his available manpower, with a big concentration on hard training and war exercises. The future exponents of armoured warfare like Guderian and Rommel had their formative training during von Seeckt's years, while the victors of the First World War ran down their armies and retired to peacetime soldiering.

The first tanks

National pride had to be restored in those uneasy years in Germany, and the *Reichswehr* played their part by training hard. Von Seeckt's swan song was to initiate a strictly unofficial programme of experimental tank construction. The first tank to appear was made by the firm of Rheinmetall-Borsig, in mild steel and described as a *Grosstraktor* (big tractor) – a thin disguise to circumvent the terms of the Treaty. The vehicle was similar in layout to the contemporary British Medium Mk II tank, weighed around 20 tons and had a 75-mm gun. A year later, in 1927, the firm produced a smaller version of the same thing, called a

Leichtetraktor (light tractor), this time with a 37-mm gun. A second vehicle of the same type was fitted with a 75-mm gun, and in 1929 there was an improved version, weighing around 10 tons and with the same 37-mm gun and turret as the 1927 model.

These early vehicles gave design experience and were tested secretly in western Russia (with Russian co-operation) at a Soviet tank school, so that strictly speaking they were not contravening the Versailles Treaty terms. Meanwhile tactical experience was gained on *Reichswehr* exercises by the use of dummy tanks, and Major Heinz Guderian, who was a staff tactical instructor at the *Reichswehr's* motor transport school, is credited with the idea. He had dummy tank outlines fabricated from sheet metal and wood, and attached to the BMW Dixi light car which was then a standard type of staff and liaison vehicle. These were supplemented by unpowered 'soapbox' dummies on wheels which were pushed around by men inside them, rather like carnival floats.

Keen disciple

Guderian was a keen disciple of the writings of Captain B H Liddell-Hart, the distinguished British military commentator of the 1920s and 1930s, and of Major-

General J F Fuller and other leading British tank warfare theorists who had had experience in the Royal Tank Corps in 1917/18. While in Britain these theorists had only limited success in seeing their ideas realised – for a variety of reasons which included a conservative outlook by the General Staff and a severely limited defence budget – their views were keenly studied by Guderian. In 1931 Guderian, by then a Lieutenant-Colonel, became Chief of Staff to General Lutz, Inspector of Motorised Troops. Lutz and Guderian were convinced that the future tactical development of tank forces should involve the formation of Armoured (Panzer) Divisions. As far as tanks were concerned they postulated the development of two types, a medium tank in the 20-ton class, armed with a 75-mm gun in the turret and two machine-guns, for tank-to-tank battles, and a lighter vehicle intended primarily for reconnaissance, armed with a 50-mm armour-piercing gun and two machine-guns. These conclusions were accepted by the General Staff, except for the gun on the lighter tank which was changed to 37-mm, because this was the size of gun with which the German infantry were already being equipped for the anti-tank role. The Chief of the Ordnance Office and

The first German tank, an A7V of 1918 with its crew. Inset: A dummy tank mounted on a car chassis, used for practising the Blitzkrieg techniques of the future

the Inspector of Artillery favoured the 37-mm gun and the desirability of standardisation enhanced the argument.

By this time further Rheinmetall prototypes had been built, notably a large multi-turreted vehicle known as NbFz A (*Neubaufahrzeug* [new model] A). This was clearly influenced by the British 'Independent' (a very large one-off vehicle) and the Medium Mk III, the NbFz A being quite close in size and layout to the latter. However, none of the experimental models was considered completely suitable to fill the two roles in the proposed Panzer Divisions. New models were necessary, and these eventually emerged as the PzKpfw III and IV, described later.

Until they were ready, which would take several years, a training tank was needed. In the interests of speedy production and for AFV experience a light tank was the obvious answer. Light tanks were cheap and

could be built easily, a fact already realised and one which influenced tank development in most other countries. Accordingly the Germans bought a British Carden-Loyd Mark VI chassis which was sold commercially to several powers in the 1930s. The German purchase was announced as being for use as a carrier for a 20-mm anti-aircraft gun. This modest acquisition created no undue alarm in other countries.

Keen competition
In pursuance of the new tank policy, the German Army Weapons Branch (*Heereswaffenamt*) issued a requirement for a tank of approximately five tons weight with two machine-guns mounted in a turret with all-round traverse and protected by armour immune to attack by small arms fire. Five firms, Rheinmetall-Borsig, Daimler-Benz, MAN, Henschel and Krupp were invited to submit their proposals for a design to meet

the specification. Germany was lucky to have so many firms with the necessary engineering experience and design staff. But in these relatively lean economic times there was keen competition.

After close scrutiny, LKA1, a design submitted by Krupp and based on the imported Carden-Loyd Mk VI chassis was selected, and Krupp were made responsible for the development of the chassis, while Daimler-Benz were to construct the turret and the hull. To ensure secrecy and to hide the project from the outside world, the machine was given the totally fictitious code name of *Landwirtschaftlicher Schlepper* (agricultural tractor), abbreviated as La S. The drawings and design were finished in December 1933, by which time Hitler and the Nazi Party had assumed power and were about to overturn openly all the terms of the Versailles Treaty. Henschel were given orders to construct three La S prototypes.

LKA 1 (above left)
Krupp's prototype for a five-ton light tank was designed to meet the needs of the rearming *Reichswehr* in 1933. Accepted for trials, this vehicle was the forerunner of the PzKpfw I

PzKpfw I Ausf A
The Panzer I A was tested during the Spanish Civil War, and saw service during Hitler's early Blitzkriegs
  Engine: 60 hp Krupp M105 *Weight:* 5·4 tons
Speed: 25 mph *Crew:* 2 *Armour:* 13 mm max
Armament: 2 × 7·92-mm mg

The first of the vehicles ran in February 1934, an extremely short period even allowing for the fact that the tank was a very simple one with a derived chassis.

Full-scale production began in 1934 with an order for 150 machines given to Henschel under the designation 1A La S Krupp, and this was followed by another version known as 1B La S. About 1800 vehicles in all were built and of these roughly 1500 were the B model, longer and with a more powerful engine.

The La S designation was retained until 1938 when the Germans introduced a new standard code for tank designation. Experimental machines were given an identifying serial number – 700 or 2000 for example. The first number or pair of numbers indicated the weight class of the vehicle, eg 7-ton or 20-ton or 30-ton. The last two numbers were used to indicate the number of the prototype. A prefix VK indicated that the vehicle was fully tracked and where a multiple order had been given to competing firms, the firm's initial letters followed in a bracket after the serial number, eg VK

2001 (H) and VK 2002 (DB) would indicate tanks in the 20-ton class under experimental construction by Henschel and Daimler-Benz respectively.

Designating the panzers
When a tank had been accepted for service it became known by its class name followed by the model number. *Panzerkampfwagen*, abbreviated into PzKpfw or PzKw, was used. For example, PzKpfw I Ausf C indicated Model C of the first tank type. On acceptance into the service a tank also received an Ordnance Dept inventory number, eg *Sonderkraftfahrzeug* (special motor vehicle) 101, abbreviated to SdKfz 101.

The PzKpfw I Ausf A (SdKfz 101) was a straightforward machine with no unexpected characteristics or technical devices. Its 3·5 litre air-cooled Krupp M 305 four-cylinder petrol (gasoline) engine developed 57 hp at 2500 rpm and was housed in the engine compartment at the back of the tank together with a large oil cooler. The drive was taken forward to a five-speed sliding pinion gearbox and thence through cross shafts, carrying on each side a clutch and brake steering system, to the front driving sprockets. Several machines were fitted with the Krupp M 601 diesel engine which developed 45 hp at 2200 rpm, but the experiment proved unsuccessful and the Krupp petrol engine was used in all production models of the PzKpfw I Ausf A.

Refining the suspension

Krupp's original prototype had four suspension wheels each side with a rear idler touching the ground; movement of the wheels was controlled by coil springs and three return rollers were mounted on the hull. The layout was changed in the production models, which had an external girder covering the two rear suspension wheels. The ends of this girder were connected to the axle of the second suspension wheel and to the rear idler wheel axle by forked links carrying elliptical springs whose tips rested on the axles of the third and fourth suspension wheels. Movement of the leading suspension wheel was controlled by coil springs and three return rollers were mounted on the hull. The suspension was satisfactory at low speeds but pitched badly when the tank was moving faster, probably accentuated by the rear idler wheel which remained in contact with the ground. The overall length was, in round figures, 14 ft, the width 6 ft 10 in and the height 5 ft 8 in. This was indeed a small tank. The vehicle, however, was very versatile and with its two 7·92-mm machine-guns could give a good account of itself. The armament consisted of MG 34s, although it is quite possible that tanks of early manufacture were armed with old MG 13s, taking as evidence some pre-war photographs.

Evolved from the Ausf A, the PzKpfw Ausf B (SdKfz 101) prototype appeared in 1935. Superficially the appearance was the same, but there were considerable differences in detail. A more powerful engine, a water-cooled Maybach NL 38 TR, was installed and this required a longer and higher engine compartment. The tank was lengthened to provide the extra room and the sides of the superstructure were raised. The engine developed 100 hp at 3000 rpm and this extra power raised the speed of the tank from 23 to 25 mph

The armament remained the same as in the Ausf A and despite the many disadvantages the two-man crew was retained. Armour thickness remained at 13 mm and the turret showed no change except that an internal mantlet was used, a design feature that appeared on all German tanks until the introduction of the 50-mm gun on the PzKpfw III. In 1940/41 a redesigned transmission incorporating a five-speed gearbox and a better final drive reduction gear was substituted for the type in the Ausf A. The nose of the tank was redesigned to provide room for the final reduction gear which resulted in a complicated design pattern for casting. In both the Ausf A and B no special provision was made for observation by the commander who was, of course, the gunner as well.

To allow for the extra room needed by the bigger engine in the Ausf B the suspension was modified and an extra wheel, making five in all, was added on each side. The rear idler wheel was raised clear of the ground which greatly improved the ride, and the additional suspension wheel meant that the same amount of track as before was in contact with the ground. Four return rollers were used on the hull in place of the three of the earlier model.

The turret was set over on the right hand side of the superstructure; the driver sat on

General Heinz Guderian, one of the early prophets of armoured warfare, and one of the outstanding tank leaders of the Second World War

the left hand side of the hull. This gave a wider hull with the tracks a little further apart and therefore the tank possessed rather more lateral stability than most contemporary light tanks.

VK 1801

1940 prototype for the PzKpfw I *neuer Art* (new model) featured heavier armour as an infantry support vehicle. Thirty of the type were built
Engine: 150 hp Maybach HL 45 *Weight:* 18·5 tons *Speed:* 15 mph *Crew:* 2 *Armour:* 82 mm max *Armament:* 2 × 7·92-mm mg (never fitted)

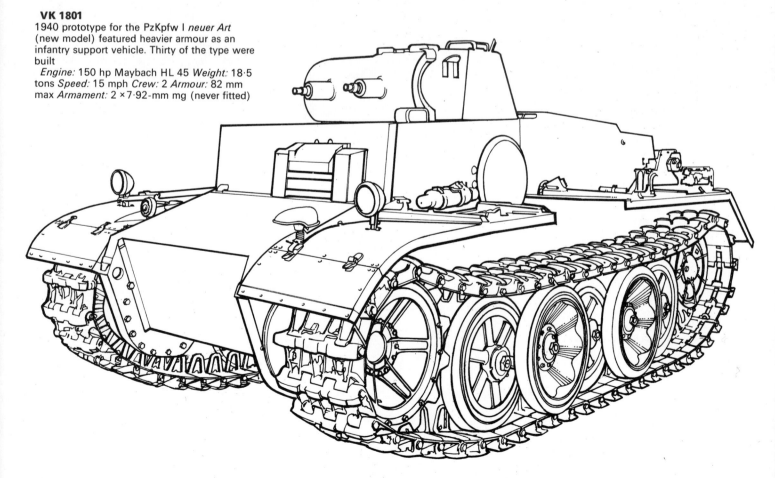

TRIAL BY COMBAT

Columns of tanks looked impressive on the parade-ground, but a propaganda show of strength was a long way from the realities of war. The fledgling weapon needed the chance to test tactics and hardware. The Spanish Civil War presented that opportunity. Above: PzKpfw I Ausf A in Catalonia, 1938

Both models of the Panzer I were 'blooded' in the Spanish Civil War (1936–1939). In this war, the Germans had seen the opportunity to test many of their new weapons. Here were the real battles and along with the Condor Legion, the Panzer I was put to the test. But from observations in Spain it became clear that tanks with far heavier weapons, better armour and longer endurance would be necessary for a future war of mobility.

Guderian was largely responsible for planning the whole complementary series of tanks to equip the new Panzer Division. He postulated a light reconnaissance tank, and a major medium battle tank (ultimately known as the PzKpfw III) which would be fitted with an armour-piercing gun as well as hull and turret machine-guns. The other major type (later to be known as the PzKpfw IV) would be a support vehicle with a 75-mm low velocity gun. Development of the Panzer III and IV proceeded more slowly than forecast. To cover the delay in getting these tanks into the hands of troops it was decided to build a tank in the 10-ton class as a successor

to the Panzer I. The new tank was intended to be a training machine stop-gap; it was used in the Spanish Civil War and in the opening stages of the Second World War, being important in the 1939/40 period.

A specification for the new design was issued in July 1934. Three prototypes were submitted, one of them being Krupp's LKA II which looked quite like their prototype LKA I for the PzKpfw I. Prototypes were also built by Henschel and MAN, both resembling the Krupp design except for radical differences in the suspension;

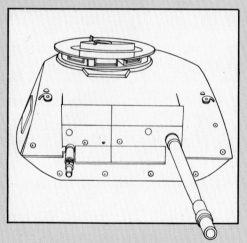

LKA II
Krupp's prototype for the PzKpfw II closely resembled their LKA I. It was rejected in favour of the MAN proposal

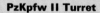

PzKpfw II Turret
Retaining the layout of 20-mm cannon and co-axial MG 34 7·92-mm machine-gun, the later model Panzer II turrets were equipped with an all-round periscope cupola

PzKpfw II Ausf A on the Western Front in 1940

with the designation La S 100, the MAN vehicle was selected for production.

Twenty-five tanks were built in 1935 as 1 La S 100 and taken into service as PzKpfw II Ausf a1 (SdKfz 121). They weighed 7·2 tons, had a crew of three and were armed with a 20-mm KwK 30 gun and a 7·92-mm machine-gun mounted coaxially in the turret. The vehicle was powered by a Maybach HL 57 six-cylinder petrol engine developing 130 hp at 2100 rpm. A plate clutch and a six-speed gearbox took the power to a cross shaft; this carried at either end the usual clutch and brake steering mechanism for each track and a driving sprocket. The suspension consisted of six small road wheels in pairs in bogies which were sprung by leaf springs. An outside girder connected the outer ends of the bogie pivot pins, the inboard ends being housed in the hull which

also carried three return rollers. The adjustable rear idler wheel was clear of the ground. The nose plate was a rounded casting, a distinct change from previous German tanks.

These 25 vehicles were followed, also in 1935, by a second batch of 25 PzKpfw II Ausf a2. Externally they were exactly the same as the Ausf a1 but had a better cooling system and more room had been found in the engine compartment. A further batch of 50 machines appeared in 1936 – the PzKpfw II Ausf a3. Further improvements had been effected in the cooling system and the tracks and suspension had been altered for the better in comparison with the earlier machines.

The 2/La S 100, or PzKpfw II Ausf b, appeared in 1936. One hundred machines were built with front armour increased to

30 mm and an all-up weight of 7·9 tons. The armament remained unchanged, but a Maybach HL 62 petrol engine was fitted which developed 140 hp. Externally there was little change. These tanks had a new reduction gear in the cross drive and a new type of driving sprocket which incorporated a geared final drive. These sprockets, together with new pattern track plates that appeared with the machine, were adopted as standard fittings for all subsequent PzKpfw IIs.

In 1937 the third version, 3/La S 100 or PzKpfw II Ausf c, appeared. Slight alterations were made to the turret, which still housed the same 20-mm Solothurn armament, and the driver's front plate extended right across the tank. In other models the superstructure sides tapered slightly towards the front and the driver's plate was narrower than the width of the hull. A

PzKpfw II Ausf B or C

Ausf B and C of the Panzer II were virtually unchanged from the Ausf A, except that the commander was provided with a cupola instead of a periscope. Panzer IIs of all three marks suffered a terrible mauling in Russia in 1941
Engine: 140 hp Maybach HL TR *Weight:* 9·5 tons *Speed:* 25 mph *Crew:* 3 *Armour:* 30 mm max *Armament:* 20-mm cannon; 1 mg

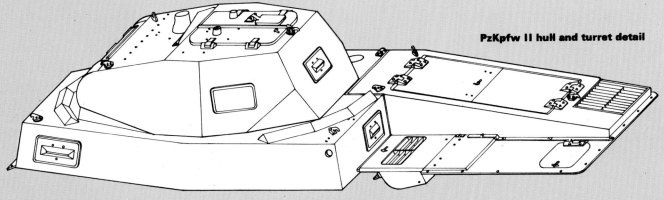

PzKpfw II hull and turret detail

radical change had been effected in the suspension. The outside girder and the small bogies disappeared and were replaced by five medium-sized suspension wheels each individually controlled by quarter elliptic springs. Four return rollers were used on the hull. This suspension was used for all following models of PzKpfw II.

The early versions of the PzKpfw II were tried out under operational conditions in the Spanish Civil War. The performance of the vehicles showed that though they were only intended as training machines they were well made and could play their part in armoured warfare provided that the opposition was not too strong, but even against the primitive anti-tank guns encountered in Spain the Panzer IIs were virtually outclassed. It would appear that the vulnerability of the German tanks during the war

in Spain was somewhat overlooked by the German General Staff who went ahead and approved the continued large-scale production of the PzKpfw II which by 1938/39 was on the way to becoming obsolescent. Even though its armour was increased it was barely proof against the current anti-tank guns in Europe, such as the British 2-pounder. While the armament was adequate for taking on its own kind, the PzKpfw II was too weakly armed and armoured to deal with heavier hostile tanks and could not fire HE (High Explosive) shot. However, despite these shortcomings – which were well known to all German Panzer officers – production continued well into 1942.

The PzKpfw II Ausf A, B and C appeared between 1937 and 1940. There was little difference between these models. The 1937 tanks which marked the start of real mass

production showed little change from PzKpfw II Ausf c. To improve protection the nose plate was changed and became angular and of welded construction instead of being round in shape and cast in construction. The gun mantlets were very slightly changed with flanges at the top and bottom of the internal moving shield, to reduce shot splash. The turret was otherwise unchanged except that provision was now made for a commander's periscope in the Model A and a cupola in Model B and subsequent models.

The German Army had 955 PzKpfw IIs for the attack on France in May 1940, and 1067 when the Russian campaign began in 1941. By April 1942 this had been reduced to 866 largely because of the vulnerability of these small tanks against superior Russian machines.

Notwithstanding the considerable effort made in the late 1930s to equip the Panzer Divisions with effective vehicles, the outbreak of war in September 1939 found the Germans woefully short of their intended AFV (Armoured Fighting Vehicle) establishment. Popular myth – which was to a great extent created by clever German propaganda – has left to this day the legend that the Panzer Divisions which stormed into Poland in 1939, and France and Flanders in 1940, were a vast and unstoppable armoured force. But the truth is that it was only the acquisition of the entire Czechoslovak arms industry after the Munich Agreement of 1938 which gave the German forces sufficient tanks with which to put an adequate Panzer Army into the field.

Armaments firms in Czechoslovakia, prior to the occupation by Germany in March 1939, were concerned with the design, development and production of tanks and other armoured fighting vehicles – both for use by the Czech Army and for commercial sale to foreign armies. The two main tank models were the Skoda LT-35 and the CKD (*Cesko-moravska Kolben Danek*) TNHP, which the Germans took into service as the PzKpfw 35(t) and the PzKpfw 38(t) respectively, the t being an abbreviation of *tscheche*, the German for Czech.

In 1933 the CKD firm of Prague began the design of a new light tank series intended for export. This model received the factory designation LT (Light Tank) L and was subsequently called the TNHB. For export purposes it was often referred to as the LT-34.

During October 1937 the Czech Defence Department formed a tank evaluation committee to conduct thorough testing of all available Czech tank designs. A new tank testing centre was established outside the factory during January 1938. Several factories submitted vehicles for tests apart from CKD, among these being the famous Skoda firm and the lesser known Adamov firm. By this time the CKD LTL-H series had resulted in the LTL-P (TNHS) model with improved armament and armour. Results of the trials showed the TNHS to be the most exceptional model of those submitted and after a gruelling 3000-mile test, some 1000 miles of which were across country, the tank showed virtually no mechanical defects. Throughout its life this tank chassis earned great respect for its reliability and durability. The maintenance and servicing needed were found to be minimal and could be carried out in the field.

Following a report on these tests the

The Czech tanks: a great arms industry falls into Hitler's hands

Czech Defence Department specified that the TNHS should enter production and become the standard tank of the Army. Orders were issued for 150 vehicles. After alteration the new tank was given the designation TNHP.

Export models

Prior to, and during the course of, the tests by the Czech Army, CKD had received orders for most of the developed models from foreign governments. These included Sweden, Switzerland, Peru, Latvia, Yugoslavia and Afghanistan. A total of 196 tanks of this series was exported. One vehicle was purchased by the War Mechanisation Board in Great Britain, who tested it extensively.

The original 8-ton tank mounted a 37·2-mm tank gun (Model Skoda A7) L/47·8 and a coaxial 7·92-mm Besa machine-gun in a turret with all-round traverse. The bulge

at the rear of the turret was fitted for ammunition stowage. A further 7·92-mm Besa machine-gun (a British-designed weapon) was ball-mounted at the front of the hull. The elevation gear of the 37-mm gun could be locked for firing and it was intended to fire only when the vehicle was stationary. The coaxial 7·92-mm machine-gun could be used independently when required, by virtue of its ball mounting.

The traversing gear, which was fast and light in action, was operated by a wheel on the left hand side of the gunner. It could be thrown out of action and the turret could then be pushed round by the gunner. The turret ring was 47·5 inches in internal diameter and there was no turntable or turret basket. The cupola, which was fixed, was replaceable with 4 periscopes, each with mirrors and protective glasses. The forward machine-gun could be operated if

necessary by the driver, via a Bowden cable attached to one of the steering levers. Construction was riveted with the exception of the top of the superstructure which was bolted. Protection was 25 mm basis at the front, 19 mm on the sides, and 15 mm on the rear.

Four rubber-tyred single wheels were provided on each side, each wheel being mounted on a cranked stub-axle and each pair of wheels being controlled by a semi-elliptic spring freely pivoted. There were two return rollers on each side, mounted well forward. Front sprocket drive was employed, the sprocket being mounted high off the ground. The tracks were engaged by twin sprockets and each sprocket was driven through an internally toothed gear by a pinion attached to the cross shaft. The cross shaft carried two steering units comprising epicyclic and clutch elements giving

PzKpfw 35(t)
Power steering and gear change made this an exceptionally easy tank to steer. It could also achieve remarkably high cross-country speeds. Only a few hundred were used by the Wehrmacht. Left: A 35(t) in France, 1940
Engine: 120 hp ohv *Weight:* 9·9 tons
Speed: 25 mph *Crew:* 4 *Armour:* 35 mm max
Armament: 37·2-mm Skoda L/40; 2 × 7·92-mm mg

two steering ratios and was driven by a bevel gear from an epicyclic five-speed gearbox situated between the driver on the right and the machine-gunner on the left. The forward end of the vehicle was therefore quite congested.

The propeller shaft passed through the centre of the fighting compartment, and a six-cylinder, water-cooled, Praga TNHP ohv petrol engine (as used in commercial trucks) was mounted vertically on the centre-line of the vehicle in the rear compartment. A single dry-plate clutch was installed. The engine had a dry sump and was cooled by a finned cylinder incorporating an Auto-Klean filter. Bosch magneto ignition was employed and all the sparking plugs were screened. A 12-volt dynamo was belt-driven from the crankshaft. Cooling was effected by a centrifugal fan driven through a universal joint from the crankshaft. The air was drawn partly through the bulkhead, but mainly through a mushroom type louvre over the engine compartment and thence through a radiator of the continuous fin and tube type. The air was ejected through an opening in the rear top plate protected by armour-steel slats covered by expanded metal. The fuel tanks were situated on either side of the engine compartment and the total capacity was 49 gallons. The floor plates immediately below the fuel tanks were secured by a few small-diameter bolts, the idea being that in the event of an explosion resulting from damage to the fuel tanks the floor plates would be blown out and so reduce the possibility of damage within the vehicle.

The track was made up of cast steel shoes and the pins were each secured by a clip. Detachable spuds were provided to increase track grip in snow and ice. These were located on the extremities of the pins, which projected beyond the faces of the lugs.

Commandeered by the Wehrmacht

Following the German occupation of Czechoslovakia, from 15 March 1939, all tanks in service with the Czech Army – as well as those in production under export contracts – were taken over by the Wehrmacht. The Germans designated the TNHP the PzKpfw 38(t) (37-mm) and continued its production until early 1942, when Czech tank production was suspended. Production of the vehicle under German guidance was also carried out by the Skoda firm. In 1940 the CKD firm was redesignated BMM (Böhmisch-Mährische Maschinenfabrik AG). The Germans initially requested a monthly production figure of 40 vehicles, although this fluctuated greatly according to the availability of materials and manpower. A total of 1168 tanks of this type was built for the Wehrmacht: 275 in 1940, 698 in 1941 and 195 in 1942. In 1940 228 were in service with VII and VIII Panzer Divisions. By 1 July 1941 there were 763, but this figure dropped to 522 by April 1942.

The PzKpfw 38(t) saw service with the Wehrmacht in Poland, France, Yugoslavia, Greece and Russia, and formed a major part of the tank strength of Rommel's VII Panzer Division during its drive across Northern France in the 1940 campaign. During 1940/41 the PzKpfw 38(t) formed 25% of the total German tank force and its importance was therefore considerable, the vehicle being much superior in hitting power to either the PzKpfw I or II. In 1940 a total of 90 vehicles being built for Sweden were also

Imperial War Museum

PzKpfw 38(t)

The 38(t) equipped two Panzer Divisions during the invasion of France. The proven chassis served in numerous roles throughout the war. Left: A German-built 38(t)
Engine: 125 hp ohv *Weight:* 8·5 tons
Speed: 20 mph *Crew:* 4 *Armour:* 25 mm max
Armament: 37·2-mm L/47·8; 2 × 7·2-mm mg

taken over, and these were fitted with extra radio equipment to become command tanks – designated *Panzerbefehlswagen* 38(t).

Shortly after gaining control of the Czech production facilities, the Germans ordered the manufacturers to increase the frontal armour to 50 mm and that on the sides to 30 mm. As the result, the turret front had a basic thickness of 25 mm with an additional 25-mm plate. The front vertical hull plate was similarly armoured; the side superstructure armour was 30 mm thick. (In some vehicles the Germans substituted the 37-mm KwK L/45 for the original Czech gun.) The tank's weight correspondingly increased to 11 tons. This new model became the TNHP-S (S meaning *Schwer*, or heavy).

The other Czech tank

The other Czechoslovakian tank to see service with the Panzer Divisions in the early days was what the Germans designated PzKpfw 35(t). The design of this vehicle went back to 1934 when the Skoda firm produced a

prototype 10½-ton tank, Model T-11 which was usually referred to as the LTM-35 (S II a).

Particular care was taken in the design of this vehicle to enable it to travel long distances under its own power. In addition to having a high degree of manoeuvrability considerable emphasis was placed on crew comfort and the durability of the power train. The general design requirements of this vehicle were as follows:
1 Rear sprocket drive so as to have the fighting compartment as free as possible from all power train elements
2 Engine design as short as possible so as to have a large fighting compartment
3 A six-stage transmission with an air-operated gear shift
4 Power steering through the use of compressed air so as to permit long driving hours without excessive driver fatigue
5 The suspension to be of such a design as to obtain equal pressures on all bogie wheels
6 The main accessories were to have double

installations so as to ensure a high degree of reliability and performance

Satisfactory results were achieved with the prototype and the vehicle was put into production during 1935.

The vehicle was armoured with plate up to 35 mm thick. Its armament consisted of a 37-mm gun in a traversing turret – the first Skoda tank to be fitted with one. The gun had a monobloc barrel, was semi-automatic and used a dial sight. The elevation range of the installation was from $-10°$ to $+25°$. Horizontal movement was made by hand traverse of the entire turret, while fine sighting adjustment was secured by traverse through a handwheel. This arrangement proved successful with light tanks since a counterweight at the rear of the turret balanced the gun's weight. The gun could be elevated either by direct action of the gunner's shoulder or through an elevating mechanism. At the moment of firing, however, the gun was arrested hydraulically.

A coaxial machine-gun was used as a secondary weapon. Both weapons could be fired simultaneously or individually and the dial sight of the gun was fitted with reticule scales. In addition each machine-gun had its own sighting telescope. A further machine-gun was mounted in the hull, and fired, in a similar fashion to that on the TNHP tank. The A3 gun was further modified to adapt itself to the narrow turret by shortening the recoil and modifying the elevation wheel so that it was unnecessary for the gunner to release it for firing. The gun was improved by increasing the muzzle velocity to 2620 fps. The general internal layout was otherwise similar to that of the PzKpfw 38(t).

The particular advantage in the design of this tank was the operating efficiency which reduced driver fatigue. The vehicle was very fast and easy to steer, thanks to its 12-speed gearbox and pneumatic-servomechanical steering unit. Trips of 125 miles per day at average speeds of 12–16 mph could be achieved, although the maximum speed of the vehicle was only 25 mph. The durability of the suspension was also remarkable in that track and bogie-wheel life ranged from 4000–8000 km.

This vehicle was adopted by the Wehrmacht as the PzKpfw 35(t) during 1939, and was issued to VI Panzer Division. Originally the Germans had 106 of these tanks in service. During service in the Russian winter it was found that the steering system froze, and consequently a heater was installed. When the 35(t)s were phased out of service they were used for towing purposes and were sometimes employed for tank recovery purposes with a two-man crew. These then – the PzKpfw I, the PzKpfw II, the PzKpfw 38(t) and the PzKpfw 35(t) – formed the bulk of the Panzer Division strength in the key build-up years of 1936/39. The PzKpfw III and IV were also just in service when Germany invaded Poland on 1 September 1939, but these vehicles are more appropriately covered in the next section.

EARLY HEAVY TANKS
GOOD PROPAGANDA

The German pre-war heavy tanks were all built to the same basic specification, but three different models were constructed by different companies. *Grosstraktor* I was built by Daimler-Benz, *Grosstraktor* II was built by Rheinmetall, and *Grosstraktor* III by Krupp. The vehicles were superficially similar in shape and size, although all differed in suspension and details.

For main armament, *Grosstraktor* I had a 105-mm gun and the other two a 75-mm gun. A feature of all the models was an auxiliary machine-gun turret at the rear for enfilading enemy trenches as the vehicles crossed over.

In concept the *Grosstraktor* followed the rhomboid shape of the tanks which appeared at the end of the First World War such as the Anglo-American Mk VIII, with a central traversing turret instead of sponsons containing the main armament. These tanks were only experimental and never went into production.

As a result of these experiments, plans were drawn up by 1934 for a new design of tank very similar in size and layout to the *Grosstraktor* but incorporating new features, such as auxiliary gun turrets fore and aft, in the style of contemporary Russian and British heavy tanks. Designation given

to the new design was *Neubaufahrzeug* (NbFz) or 'new construction vehicle'. Six of these vehicles were built by Rheinmetall and Krupp, and as prototypes they were all of mild steel construction.

The NbFz was powerfully armed with either 75-mm and 37-mm guns coaxially mounted (Model A), or 105-mm and 37-mm guns mounted coaxially in a vertical plane (Model B). It is believed that only one of the latter was actually built. The two auxiliary turrets each mounted twin MG 13 machine-guns. Power was provided by a 360 hp six-cylinder Maybach engine with six speeds with drive to the rear sprocket. The crew numbered seven – commander, driver, two gunners, two machine-gunners and a radio-operator. The maximum thickness of the mild steel plate was 14·5 mm. Maximum speed was about 15 mph.

In the event no order for the NbFz was ever placed, even in later years, for the equipment for the Panzer Divisions evolved into the family of four vehicles – the PzKpfw I, II, III and IV. Of these the last two were considered to be adequately armed and armoured to form the backbone of the armoured strength of the Wehrmacht and there was little need for the NbFz. A new design was thought to be more desirable as

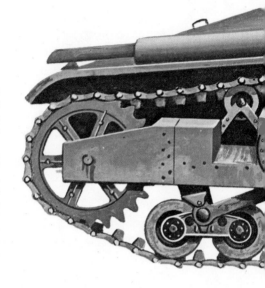

PzKpfw VI (NbFz B)
The second *Neubaufahrzeug* had as its main armament a 105-mm gun with coaxial 37-mm, with the same auxiliary turret armament as the PzKpfw V (below). Only two were built, and they were scrapped along with the model Vs in 1941

PzKpfw V (NbFz A)
The only difference between this and the PzKpfw VI were the V's main armament of a 75-mm gun with coaxial 37-mm. The 360 hp engine gave it a maximum speed of about 25 mph; maximum armour thickness was 14·5 mm; and the two auxiliary turrets each had two MG 13 machine-guns

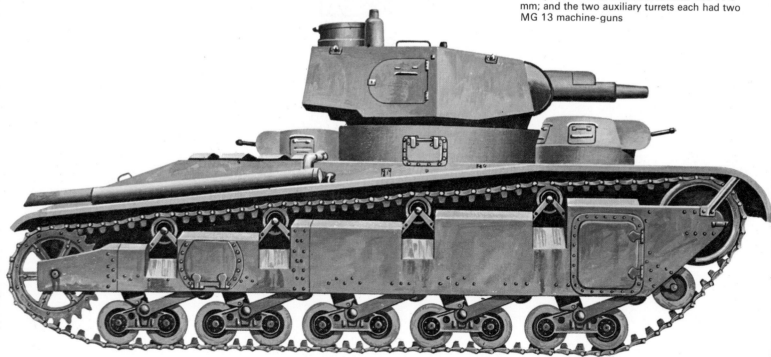

a heavier successor to the Panzer IV and this appeared as the DW I 'breakthrough' tank of 1937.

Meanwhile, in 1939, the NbFz was re-designated within the German ordnance classification as a standard design. The Model A (75-mm gun) became the PzKpfw V and the Model B (105-mm gun) became the PzKpfw VI. After the swift demise of these vehicles in 1940/41, the PzKpfw V and VI designations were transferred to the later Panther and Tiger respectively.

If the NbFz models were not to see production, they did achieve fame in 1940 as the visual symbol of German armoured might. In April of that year they were shipped to Oslo at the time of the German invasion of Norway. Five tanks were landed at Oslo docks and another at Putlos. Cleverly posed propaganda photographs of the few vehicles in existence were flashed around the world as 'heavy tanks of the German Army in Oslo', although in fact the photographs actually showed *all* the heavy tanks the Germans then possessed. After the Norwegian campaign the NbFz tanks were shipped back to Germany and disappeared into obscurity. After the war the Allies found documents ordering their scrapping in 1941. So ended the brief career of the pre-war heavy tanks. The hour belonged to two medium designs.

Propaganda photo of NbFz heavy tanks in Oslo during the German occupation of Norway, April 1940

Chris Ellis

BETTER TANKS BETTER TACTICS

The experience gained with the PzKpfw I and II led German planners to bold new concepts of design and tactics. By the outbreak of war, two finely balanced designs formed the back-bone of the Panzer Divisions which secured the Blitzkrieg victories

From 1935 onwards the collective knowledge gained during the design and development of the PzKpfw I and PzKpfw II tanks enabled the German tank-building industry to produce its own design ideas. No longer did it have to rely on foreign developments. Native ideas were, however, sometimes very complicated and did not always take into account the practical difficulties which were later encountered in mass production.

We have already seen that Guderian, the key staff officer, considered two types of armoured fighting vehicles to be required for the full strength Panzer Divisions of the future. The first was to be fitted with an armour-piercing gun as well as bow and turret machine-guns; the other, thought of as a support vehicle, was to have a larger calibre low velocity gun for support purposes. It was planned to equip the three light companies of tank battalions with the first of these two: the PzKpfw III.

Fundamental differences

There were fundamental differences of opinion on the question of arming the vehicle. The Weapons Department and the Artillery Inspectorate considered the 37-mm gun to be sufficient, while the Inspectorate for Motorised Troops demanded a 50-mm gun. The infantry was already equipped with a 37-mm anti-tank gun and, in the interests of standardisation, it was decided to use the same armour-piercing weapon in the PzKpfw III. The installation of the 50-mm gun was rejected at that time. But one provision made was that the PzKpfw III's turret ring would be of a diameter sufficiently large to make possible the fitting of a bigger calibre weapon at a future date.

The question of German road bridge limitations determined that the maximum permissible fighting weight of both the PzKpfw III and IV be 24 tons. A maximum speed of 25 mph was required. The crew was to consist of five men: commander, gun layer and loader in the turret, and driver and wireless operator in the forward compartment. The commander was to have a raised seat, between the aimer's and the loader's places in mid-turret, which would have its own cupola, allowing an all-round view. Throat microphones were to be used for communication among the crew members and also for the radio link from tank to tank, while on the move.

In 1935 The Army Weapons Branch (*Heereswaffenamt*) issued development contracts for the PzKpfw III to MAN, Daimler-Benz, Rheinmetall-Borsig, and Krupp. The Weapons Department's cover name for this vehicle was *Zugkraftwagen* (Platoon Commander's Vehicle) and from 1936 onwards the prototypes were thoroughly tested. The outcome was that Daimler-Benz were made responsible for development and production. In contrast to that of the PzKpfw IV, the PzKpfw III's suspension arrangements showed the influence of the motor car industry in that only torsion rod suspension was used from the fourth model onwards.

The selection of tank building contractors seems to have been made regardless of those manufacturers who had had experience in the mass production of vehicles. The conclusion which can be drawn from this is that, at that particular time, no mass production requirement for these tanks was foreseen. The two largest motor car firms in Germany, Ford and Opel, were deliberately excluded from the tank programme because of their American ownership.

In 1936 the first PzKpfw III tank was produced by Daimler-Benz and ten machines went for troop trials, designated as 1/ZW. Eight of these were fitted with the 37-mm gun. Although the armoured hull, housing and turret did not change substantially throughout its life, the 1/ZW suspension was of an experimental nature and consisted of five large double bogies which were hung on coil springs. The remainder of the suspension was made up of a front driving wheel and a rear idler together with two return rollers. Armour was between 5 and 14·5 mm thick and the overall weight was 15 tons. The engine installed was a development of the Maybach DSO 12-cylinder, high performance 108 TR, which with an approximate capacity of 11 litres, produced a maximum power of 250 hp and a top speed of 20 mph. Transmission was a ZF SFG 75, five gear drive. A total of 150 rounds was carried for the main armament and 4500 rounds for the three machine-guns, two of which were co-axial to the main armament, in the turret. This vehicle was known unofficially as the PzKpfw III Ausf A.

New models

Models B and C appeared during 1937. A new suspension system was tried on these, consisting of eight small bogie wheels on longitudinal leaf springs, and return rollers were increased to three. Armament remained the 37-mm tank gun L/45 in an internal mantlet with two MG 34s, while a third machine-gun, fitted into the front compartment, was worked by the wireless operator. Fifteen each of the Ausf B model (type 2/ZW) and the Ausf C model (type 3a/ZW) were constructed. Armour thickness remained constant at 14·5 mm all round.

The Ausf D version (type 3b/ZW), which finally went into quantity production appeared at the end of 1938. The same suspension was retained, but the armour was increased to 30 mm all round, thus raising the total weight to about 19 tons. A slightly improved transmission was used. From the Ausf E onwards the more powerful Maybach 12-cylinder HL 120 TR, was fitted which increased the maximum output to 320 hp by enlarging the bore and increasing the cylinder capacity to 11·9 litres. The gearbox in this machine was the Maybach Variorex pre-selector with ten forward and one reverse speeds. This complicated transmission was intended to make gear changing easier, as the change was carried out by a vacuum after the gear had been pre-selected and the release valve was activated by depressing the clutch pedal. The ninth and tenth gear positions were overdrives. Top speed was 25 mph. Fifty-five examples of this version were produced, but the PzKpfw III was still only at 'troop trial' stage when the Blitzkrieg on Poland began on 1 September 1939. All the pre-production machines (Models A–D) were used in the campaign if in only nominal numbers: nevertheless valuable combat experience was gained.

Into production

It was not until 27 September 1939, that the Wehrmacht officially announced that '. . . the *Panzerkampfwagen* III (37-mm) (SdKfz 141), has been adopted for service as a result of its successful troop trials'. Mass production was started just as quickly as a scheme could be set up. With Germany now in a state of war, and with firm official control, a consortium of companies was contracted for the work. These included such famous names as Alkett (one factory on assembly, one fabricating hulls), Daimler-Benz, FAMO, Henschel, MAN, MIAG and others.

The first full production type, Ausf (Model) E (or 4/ZW), had the final type of hull shape and suspension which changed only in detail from then on. The first vehicles came off the line in late 1939 and were in service by spring 1940. There were now six bogies on each side mounted on torsion bars fitted across the hull. The vehicle weighed about 19·5 tons, had an armour basis of 30 mm and retained the Maybach HL 120 TR engine of the later pre-production machines. The hull alone weighed 13·8 tons. The coupled machine-guns (MG 34s) in the turret which had previously been coaxial with the main armament were replaced with a single

PzKpfw III Torsion Bar Suspension (right)
Used on Panzer IIIs from the Ausf E onwards, this ingenious suspension system relied on the tensile strength of an anchored metal bar to float the armoured vehicle's weight

PzKpfw III Ausf B or C
Only 15 each of these models were built, in 1937, with a new leaf spring suspension system. A third machine-gun was fitted for the wireless operator in the front compartment

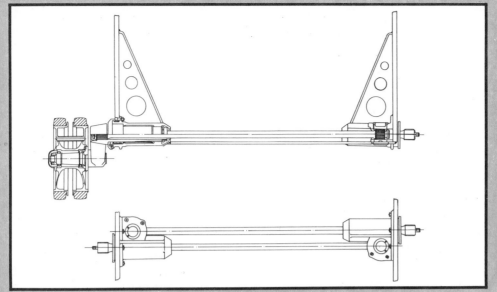

PzKpfw III Ausf E
The first mass-produced version of the Panzer III
established the basic torsion bar suspension
system and hull configuration for the rest of the
series
Engine: Maybach HL 120 TR *Weight:* 19·5 tons
Speed: 25 mph *Crew:* 5 *Armour:* 30 mm basic
Armament: 37-mm KwK L/45; 2 mg

PzKpfw III Ausf A
Ten Ausf As were produced by Daimler-Benz in
1936 with an experimental coil spring suspension
system. Most other features of the vehicle were
standard for the series
Engine: 250 hp Maybach HL 108 TR *Weight:*
15 tons *Speed:* 20 mph *Crew:* 5 *Armour:* 14·5
mm max *Armament:* 37-mm KwK L/45; 3 mg

machine-gun, but some early Ausf E machines retained the pre-production type
turrets with internal mantlet and two
machine-guns.

However, on the production type turret
the 37-mm tank gun mantlet was now
external. By early 1940 one hundred of
these machines had been built and they
were rushed into service to provide the
main hitting power of tank regiments, which
until then had to make do with the PzKpfw I
and II and the ex-Czech vehicles. Industry
could still only produce tanks in limited
numbers, and this low production capacity
became more and more of a problem until
experience was gained and manufacturing
techniques became streamlined. For the big
attack on France and Flanders on 10 May
1940, a total of only 349 PzKpfw IIIs of all
kinds was available, including the pre-
production vehicles which had been brought
back from Poland.

Improved models
If the vehicles were few and slow in
coming, there was no lack of ideas and
foresight at staff level. As early as January
1938 the Weapons Department were asked
by *Heereswaffenamt* to improve on the basic
model and re-arm it with a 50-mm tank gun.
Daimler-Benz built a prototype hull and
Krupp designed an improved turret. It was
proposed to install the 50-mm KwK L/42
with a muzzle velocity of 2250 fps against the
37-mm gun's 1475 fps. Vehicles equipped
with the new 50-mm gun were already coming off the line in May 1940 and a few saw
service before the end of the campaign in
France.

The improved vehicle was designated
PzKpfw III Ausf F and included a slightly
up-rated engine. A somewhat lower commander's cupola was a distinctive new
feature, as was a prominent equipment box
on the back of the turret. From this version
on the idler wheels were also distinctively
altered to simplify production, in that the
new idler was spoked. Some 450 examples of
this model were produced. By November
1940, moreover, the production output of
PzKpfw III had built up to about 100
vehicles per month.

In October 1940 a new model appeared, the
PzKpfw III Ausf G, and in quantitative
terms it finally became the real backbone of
the tank regiments. For North African
service special radiators and air filters were
used. These *Fiefel* filters, partly protected
by armour, were fitted to the exterior of the
engine compartment. Vehicles with this
sort of equipment received the designation
Tp (Tropical) and were the mainstay of
Rommel's famed Afrika Korps. The PzKpfw
III was also the main type of German tank
used during the fighting in Yugoslavia and
Greece in 1941. About 450 Model Gs were
constructed and altogether a total of 2143
Panzer IIIs of all types was produced during
the years 1940 and 1941.

Hitler himself took a great personal
interest in armaments of all kinds, tanks
and guns especially, perhaps a legacy of his
own days as a ranker in the trenches during
the First World War. Some of Hitler's own
ideas were practical and sensible and made a
worthwhile contribution to development as
far as armoured fighting vehicles were concerned. As we will see later, however, he
could also stubbornly force through ideas
against the better judgment of his technical
advisers at *Heereswaffenamt*, often with
perverse or wasteful results.

However, in the case of the Panzer III, Hitler was somewhat ahead of his technical advisers. Aside from sanctioning Guderian's ideas in the pre-war years, he foresaw the need to keep constantly ahead of technical development of arms and armour in enemy countries. For, despite the myth of invincibility, the quality of equipment in the first few Panzer Divisions involved in the Polish and French campaigns was relatively poor. The tanks were mostly the small pre-war types and, apart from the élite divisions (which were the ones most publicised in contemporary photographs), much of the German Army still depended heavily on horses or commandeered commercial trucks for their transport.

What was superior was the tactics. Guderian and Kleist, along with a number of brilliant divisional generals – notably Erwin Rommel, commanding VII Panzer Division – in May 1940 overthrew all the conventions of static warfare for which the Allies on the Western Front were best prepared during the 'Phoney War' period of spring 1940.

A chink in the armour

Here and there, however, there was, almost literally, a 'chink in the armour'. In the right conditions, and properly deployed, the few suitable battle tanks available to the British Expeditionary Force were more than a match for the German AFVs. This was vividly demonstrated when the Matildas of the British 1st Tank Brigade gave elements of Rommel's VII Panzers a particularly bloody nose during a counterattack at Arras on 21 May 1940. Much of the opposition proved to be light tanks and halftracks; nevertheless, Rommel recorded the loss of three of his precious Panzer IIIs and six Panzer IVs, while the British Brigade Commander later reported that one Matilda took as many as 14 hits from German 37-mm tank or anti-tank guns with only some gouging out of the armour plate to show for it. The Matilda was admittedly exceptionally well armoured for its day, though lacking in speed and size, but this action, and the Matilda's invincibility in Wavell's Libyan Campaign of late 1940, was clearly a pointer to improvements to be desired in future German tanks.

Britain was by this time known to be pressing on with development of a 6-pounder (57-mm) anti-tank gun, and by the time Rommel's Afrika Korps had become involved in the Libyan fighting there was an instruction from Field Marshal Keitel to the Army High Command, dated 7 July 1941, stating: 'The Führer considers it advantageous to up-armour our new production tanks, by fitting spaced armour plates, additional to the main armour, and thereby to neutralise the increased penetrating power of the British weapons. The increase in weight and the loss of speed must, in the Führer's opinion, be accepted.' Hitler had drawn his own conclusion and this time was right.

Meanwhile the PzKpfw III Ausf H had already appeared in late 1940, with stronger suspension and wider track width (from 360 mm to 400 mm). The hull now weighed 15·8 tons and the fighting weight had risen to 21·6 tons, while the complicated Maybach Variorex drive was replaced by a normal six gear drive with syncromesh gear box and dry plate clutch. The 50-mm L/42 gun was retained, although Hitler had, in fact, suggested when the 50-mm gun was first

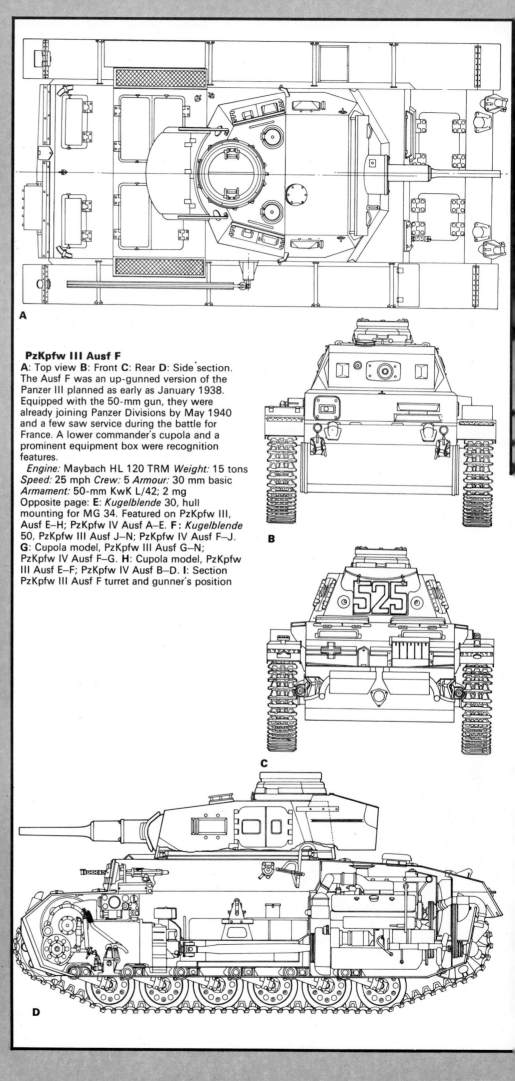

PzKpfw III Ausf F
A: Top view B: Front C: Rear D: Side section. The Ausf F was an up-gunned version of the Panzer III planned as early as January 1938. Equipped with the 50-mm gun, they were already joining Panzer Divisions by May 1940 and a few saw service during the battle for France. A lower commander's cupola and a prominent equipment box were recognition features.
Engine: Maybach HL 120 TRM *Weight:* 15 tons *Speed:* 25 mph *Crew:* 5 *Armour:* 30 mm basic *Armament:* 50-mm KwK L/42; 2 mg
Opposite page: **E**: *Kugelblende* 30, hull mounting for MG 34. Featured on PzKpfw III, Ausf E–H; PzKpfw IV Ausf A–E. **F**: *Kugelblende* 50, PzKpfw III Ausf J–N; PzKpfw IV Ausf F–J. **G**: Cupola model, PzKpfw III Ausf G–N; PzKpfw IV Ausf F–G. **H**: Cupola model, PzKpfw III Ausf E–F; PzKpfw IV Ausf B–D. **I**: Section PzKpfw III Ausf F turret and gunner's position

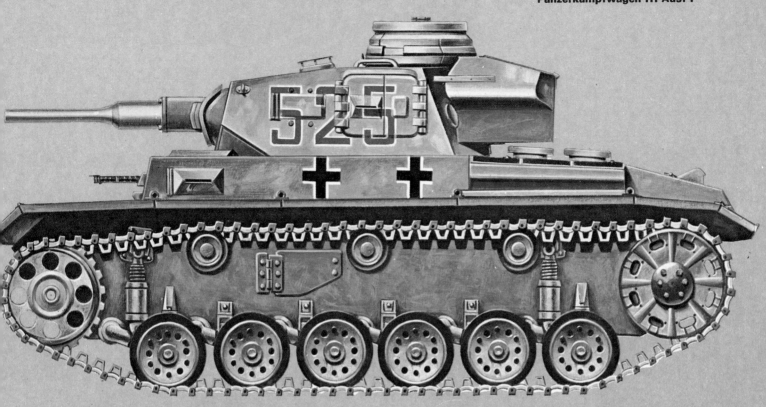

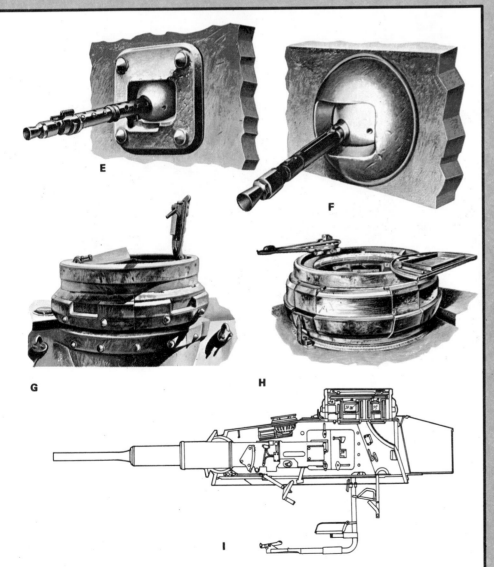

adopted for the PzKpfw III that the longer high velocity L/60 model was more desirable than the L/42 version.

However, the big inadequacies in German tank armament and armour were only fully realised in late 1941 on the Eastern Front after the appearance of the very superior Russian T-34. In July 1941 (Germany invaded Russia on 22 June 1941), the German staff estimated that 36 Panzer Divisions were needed and these would require 7992 Panzer IIIs. However, by November 1941, after the sensational battle debut of the Russian T-34, there was a complete reversal and entirely new designs of tank were being considered. At this point doubts were already being entertained as to the effectiveness of the Panzer Divisions: Hitler personally described the Panzer III as an unsuccessful design. It must, however, be made clear that, for its time, this vehicle was an extremely advanced design, and if it had been fitted with a 50-mm gun from the outset it would have been the best fighting tank in the world in 1940/41.

Better guns

In the event an order to introduce the improved L/60 50-mm gun (KwK 39) was given in 1941. Using the armour piercing *Panzergranate* 40 shell, this gun had a muzzle velocity of 3875 fps. The production version with the L/60 gun was designated PzKpfw Ausf J (SdKfz 141/1). All earlier Panzer IIIs returned to Germany for general overhaul after April 1941 and were up-gunned with this weapon, though this meant that only 78 rounds could be carried, against the 99 rounds which could be carried for the 50-mm L/42. Certain small technical differences distinguished the Ausf J from its predecessors. The reverse gear change, for instance, was originally pedal operated, but from the Ausf J onwards a hand lever was used. The internal expanding brakes, too, for this and for subsequent versions were

Top: PzKpfw III Ausf L with long 50-mm gun and spaced frontal armour. Opposite page: PzKpfw IV Ausf D shoots its accompanying infantry into a blazing Russian village

PzKpfw III Ausf L
Further refinement of the basic Panzer III produced the Ausf L, incorporating the long 50-mm KwK 39 L/60 main armament of the Ausf J. Ammunition supply was increased, and 20-mm spaced armour plate protection was provided for the driver and on the turret front

Spaced Armour Principle
Hollow charge ammunition exploded against armour plate, blasting a stream of gas and molten metal through it. Spaced armour aimed to explode the projectile against the outer layer, dissipating the blast harmlessly against the inner

concentric rather than eccentric. There were several other detail changes, and the total weight became 21·5 tons. In 1942 production figures of 150–190 vehicles a month were achieved.

The PzKpfw III Ausf L was a further improvement introduced at the end of 1941 and had increased front turret armour and additional plates 20 mm thick in front of the turret shield and the driver's plate. Increasing the front and the turret front armour to 50 mm + 20 mm (70 mm) upped the combat weight to 22·3 tons, and the machine-gun ammunition supply was increased from 2000 to 4950 rounds.

At this point we must consider the story of the last major tank to be produced under the original Guderian plans of the 1930s. This was the vehicle originally intended for the support role – with a low velocity 75-mm gun to fire HE and smoke shells, and big enough to act as a commander's vehicle if required.

In spring 1935, Krupp, Rheinmetall, and MAN all sent in designs to fit the specification drawn up by *Heereswaffenamt*. This vehicle, in the 20-ton class, was the VK2001, known under the code or 'cover' designation of BW (*Bataillonsführer Wagen*), and the Krupp design was chosen for production. The prototype trials took place at Ulm and Kummersdorf in 1937.

Small beginnings
As with the Panzer III, some pre-production models were built in small numbers for 'troop trials'. Three models, Ausf A, B and C, had been built by 1939, and the few available vehicles took part in the Polish campaign. There was much less variety in detail of these, and the relative unimportance of the PzKpfw IV as originally conceived and ordered is demonstrated by the fact that only one contractor was involved as against eight for the PzKpfw III. Also, in the 'Blitzkrieg era' of 1939/41, there was little change in the PzKpfw IV, for in service it was fulfilling the role Guderian had envisaged for it. In the event, however, the PzKpfw IV was destined to supplant the PzKpfw III as the mainstay of the Panzer Divisions for its larger size allowed it to be more effectively up-gunned and up-armoured when the urgent need arose for a more effective answer to the new Soviet and American tanks of 1942/43. The PzKpfw IV, indeed, had the distinction of remaining in production throughout the war both as a battle tank and as a major basis (with all the

other standard types) for the dozens of self-propelled guns and tank destroyers which the Germans produced.

With the outbreak of war in 1939, the design was 'frozen' and large scale production was ordered as the PzKpfw IV Ausf D. Against the PzKpfw III, the PzKpfw IV's production was modest, as will be evident from the following numbers of PzKpfw IV on Army strength during the first three years of the war: end of 1939 – 174; end of 1940 – 386; end of 1941 – 769. In fact, the total Panzer IV production during 1941 amounted to only 480, despite an order in July 1941 which requested production of 2160 to equip the planned 36 armoured divisions. A monthly production goal of 40 per month was set for 1941, while in January 1942 a monthly output of 57 units was anticipated. In the event this target was exceeded and 964 urgently needed vehicles were produced during 1942. Originally the main assembly was by Krupp of Gruson, with hulls and turrets supplied by Krupp of Essen and Eisen of Bochum.

This picture changed considerably during 1942 due to Allied air raids. The relocation of key war industry to areas not readily accessible to the bombers was begun in 1940 and established several new tank factories. One of these was *Nibelungenwerke* at St Valentin, Austria, managed by Steyr-Daimler-Puch. Initially intended for the production of a replacement vehicle for PzKpfw IV – the Porsche *Leopard* (Porsche Type 100) – it became operational just in time to take on the expanded Panzer IV production. From 1943, the Panzer IV was assembled almost exclusively at this factory and remained in production there until the end of the war. Its proximity to the Hermann Göring steel mills at Linz established a good source of material for hulls and turrets.

The raw material used in one PzKpfw IV (without weapons, optical instruments or radio equipment) comprised 86,000 lb of steel, 2·6 lb tin, 430 lb copper, 525 lb aluminium, 140 lb lead, 146 lb zinc, $\frac{1}{3}$ lb magnesium and 256 lb rubber. These totals illustrate the enormous strain placed on German industry by tank production and go far to explain its limitations, even in the early days of the war, compared with the achievements of Allied industry in this field.

The Panzer IV hull was a comparatively simple design. All joints were austenitic steel welds and the plates were high-quality chromium-molybdenum steel made by the electric furnace process. Two bulkheads separated the hull into three compartments – driving, fighting and engine. The front driving compartment housed the transmission and final drive assemblies as well as seats for the driver and radio operator/hull gunner. Three petrol (gasoline) tanks with a capacity of approximately 105 gallons were located beneath the floor of the centre fighting compartment.

Overhanging superstructure
A most noticeable and characteristic feature of the vehicle was the superstructure, of welded construction, bolted to the top flange of the hull. To accommodate the rather large turret ring, it projected well beyond each side wall of the hull. One bolted and two hinged maintenance hatches were provided in the front glacis plate, while access hatches for driver and radio operator were provided in the roof plate, though there were many detail changes incorporated in later models.

The welded turret provided seats for three crew members – commander, gunner and loader. The sides were sloped so that the overall width was appreciably greater than

57

PzKpfw Ausf D
A: Longitudinal section B: Layout of driving,
fighting and engine compartment C: Section
through engine compartment D: Section through
fighting compartment E: Section through driving
compartment

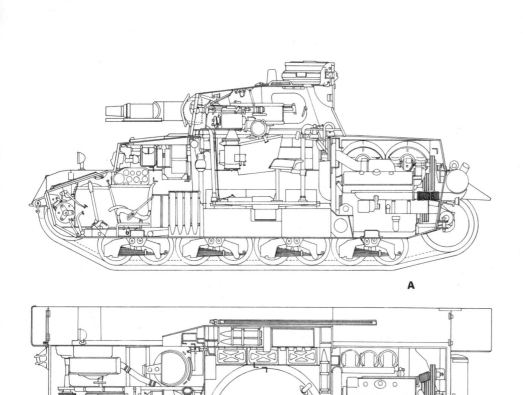

A

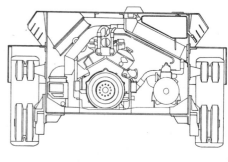

C

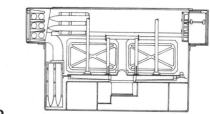

D

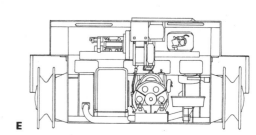

E

B

PzKpfw IV Ausf D
First produced in 1938, the Ausf D was similar
to the A, B and C models that preceded it. It
had an improved commander's cupola, better
bow machine-gun mount and various detail
changes

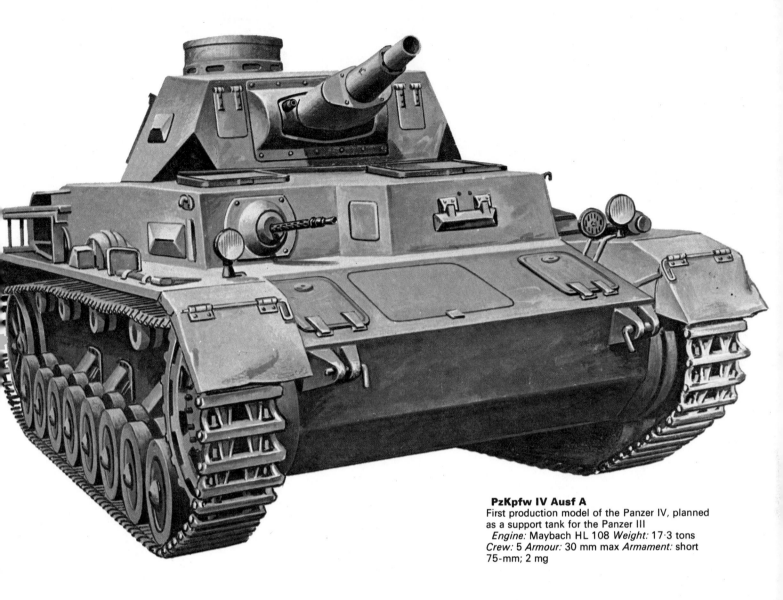

PzKpfw IV Ausf A
First production model of the Panzer IV, planned
as a support tank for the Panzer III
  Engine: Maybach HL 108 *Weight:* 17·3 tons
Crew: 5 *Armour:* 30 mm max *Armament:* short
75-mm; 2 mg

the internal diameter of the turret ring. The
75-mm gun was mounted on a trunnion axis.
The forward end of the recoil mechanism
projected through the mantlet to afford
additional protection. The commander's
cupola, set well back on the turret roof, had
five observation ports equally spaced around
it with the front port pointing directly forward in line with the gun. It was closed by a
pair of semi-circular hatch ·covers. An
observation port was provided in each side
wall of the turret, in front of the side access
hatches. Additional observation ports were
fitted at either side of the gun mantlet
officially, though these were not found on
later vehicles. A signal port was fitted on
the turret roof, similar to those mounted on
both driving compartment crew access
hatches. There were also two revolver and
carbine ports at the rear of the turret,
while the fighting compartment was venti-
lated by a roof-mounted extractor fan.

The main power plant was the standard
medium tank engine, the Maybach HL 120
TRM, a 12-cylinder, 11,867 cc liquid-cooled

petrol engine. Normally developing an
output of 300 bhp at 3000 rpm, the engine
was in most instances restricted to 2600 rpm,
giving a rating of 265 bhp. It used only low
grade 74 octane petrol. Cooling air entered
through louvres on the left hand side of the
engine compartment, was drawn through
two radiators and over the engine by two
ten-bladed fans. An exceptionally large filter
provided clean air for the power plant.

Transmission details
Engine output was transmitted by a propeller shaft and a three-plate dry clutch to
the synchro-mesh six-speed gearbox. Small
multi-disc synchronising clutches were used
for 2nd, 3rd, 4th, 5th and 6th gears. A Krupp-
Wilson 'Clutch-Brake' final drive and steering mechanism was used. In this, the input
gear drove the annulus of an epicyclic train.
The sunwheel was coupled to a steering
brake drum, which was held stationary by
an external band and compression spring
while the vehicle was in motion. The drive
from the epicyclic annulus was transmitted

through the planet carrier to the spur
reduction gears, which drove the track
sprockets. The six-speed gearbox and the
final drive units had one common oil circula-
tion system.

Each track consisted of 98 links, each 400
mm wide with 120 mm pitch. Manganese
steel was used for this 'skeleton' type of
track which weighed approximately 1400 lb.
Track tension was adjusted by a large
diameter idler wheel mounted on an eccentric axle at the rear of the vehicle. The
suspension system consisted of four bogie
units per side, each of which was fitted with
two 18·5-in diameter rubber-tyred wheels.
Quarter elliptic springs were mounted on
the underside of the leading axle arm of
each bogie. The other end of the spring
rested on a shackle pin and roller, carried
on an extension of the trailing axle arm.
Four support rollers per side completed the
suspension.

Thus it can be seen that the basic Panzer
IV was a simpler vehicle than the Panzer
III, and influenced the later IIIs.

COMMAND VEHICLES
LEADING FROM THE FRONT

Well prior to the outbreak of war, the need for command vehicles to keep up with advanced echelons in an armoured assault was foreseen. Versions of both the six-wheel and eight-wheel armoured cars, comprehensively equipped with radio and map tables, were produced, as were half-track command vehicles. But with the large-scale production of tanks and an expansion to 36 armoured divisions envisaged, command versions of tanks were felt to be necessary.

Once again the ubiquitous ZW design – the Panzer III – was used, and the earliest command vehicles of this type served in the France and Flanders campaigns of May 1940.

This first type was produced by conversion of the pre-production PzKpfw III Ausf D. The official designation was *Panzerbefehlswagen* (PzBefWg) III Ausf D. (*Panzerbefehlswagen* = armoured command vehicle). Like the armoured command car, these vehicles carried a distinctive frame aerial above the engine compartment, though this was replaced by pole-type aerials from 1943. For the defence of the five-man crew there was an MG 34. A dummy gun replaced the main armament since absence of a gun would have made its function apparent to the enemy. The major series of PzBefWeg IIIs used the Ausf E

model as a basis and appeared during 1940 as the PzBefWg III Ausf E and later there was an Ausf H version with the usual additional spaced armour plates fitted in front of the driver's plate, and extra armour on the nose. At the start of the French campaign in 1940, there were 39 *Panzerbefehlswagen* with the tank divisions. In November 1940 a production contract was put out for new vehicles of this type. It was planned to turn out a total of 10 machines per month during the first six months of 1941; the final 14 of the contract were delivered in January 1942. They saw wide service on all fronts.

Spacious interior

The absence of main armament gave plenty of interior space for a command staff but made the vehicle of only limited use on active service, and it was also necessary to make special parts. There were, however, urgent demands for command vehicles which could be produced from AFVs in use with the troops in the field. In January 1941 a development contract covering this requirement was given to Daimler-Benz, ordering a new development of the armoured command vehicle. It specified that the new design was to be equipped with a 50-mm tank gun L/42 or L/60 in a fully traversing turret (the turret was fixed in the earlier

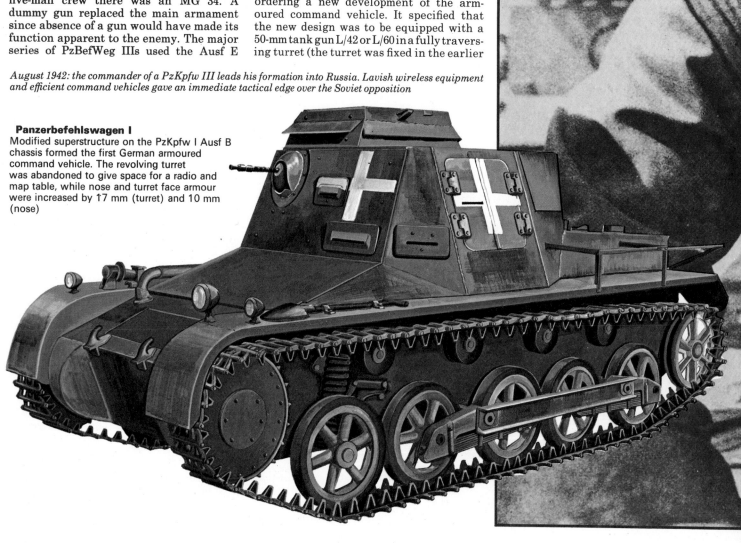

August 1942: the commander of a PzKpfw III leads his formation into Russia. Lavish wireless equipment and efficient command vehicles gave an immediate tactical edge over the Soviet opposition

Panzerbefehlswagen I
Modified superstructure on the PzKpfw I Ausf B chassis formed the first German armoured command vehicle. The revolving turret was abandoned to give space for a radio and map table, while nose and turret face armour were increased by 17 mm (turret) and 10 mm (nose)

models). Prototypes were troop tested after August 1941. The type 7/ZW hull was selected as a basis. The official designation of the new model was *Panzerbefehlswagen III Ausf K*. With a five man crew (the commander was also the wireless operator), the vehicle had a combat weight of about 23 tons. Quantity production ran from August 1942 to August 1943. The total of large and small command vehicles available on 1 July 1941 was 331 and on 1 April 1942 the total was 273.

The PzBefWg III was not the first full-tracked armoured command vehicle, however. The first German example was based on the little PzKpfw I Ausf B chassis and was built in 1939.

The superstructure was considerably modified and the sides built up to form a rectangular housing which carried a 7·92-mm MG 34 in a ball mount in the front plate for defensive purposes only. An additional 17 mm of armour plate was added to the turret face and the nose plate was also reinforced by an additional 10 mm.

Two hundred of the PzKpfw II Ausf B chassis were modified and three types were produced. Differences between them were slight, but one of them incorporated a rotating turret which was abandoned because the interior was too cramped. The crew of these tanks was increased to three men. Provision was made for a small table and for the display of maps, and two wireless sets, an Fu 2 and an Fu 6, were fitted. Additional dynamo capacity was provided.

They were first used in the Polish campaign and 96 of them were available for use in the operations in the West in 1940. Some remained in service throughout the Second World War, long after the Panzer I had disappeared from use as a fighting tank, and although the PzKpfw I and II were replaced as swiftly as PzKpfw III and IV production would allow, there were a few further developments.

PzBefWg III Ausf K had a 50-mm gun in a traversing turret and prominent aerials

A PzBefWg III armoured command vehicle fords a river during the first weeks of the invasion of Russia

AMPHIBIOUS TANKS

Bundesarchiv

PzKpfw III Ausf E equipped with snorkel and sealing devices is tested in preparation for Operation Sea Lion, the invasion of Great Britain

Some interesting other developments took place during the classic 'Blitzkrieg era'. In September and October 1940, volunteers from II Panzer Regiment at Putlos were formed into Panzer-Battalion 'A' and trained for 'Operation Sea Lion' (*Seelöwe*), the planned invasion of Great Britain. Two other special formations, Panzer Battalions 'B' and 'C', were being raised at the same time and the same place. These units later formed the XVIII Panzer Regiment of XVIII Panzer Division and converted their PzKpfw II and PzKpfw IV tanks into submersibles. All openings, vision slits, flaps, and so on, were made water tight with sealing compounds and cable tar.

The turret entry ports were bolted from the inside and the air intake opening for the engine was completely closed. A rubber cover sheet was fixed over the circular port of the tank gun, the commander's cupola and the wireless operator's machine gun. An ignition wire blew off the covering sheet upon surfacing and left the vehicle ready for action. Between the hull and the turret was a rubber sealing ring which, when inflated, prevented the water from entering.

The fresh air supply was maintained by a wire-bound rubber tube with a diameter of about 20 cm and 18 metres long. A buoy with an attached radio antenna was fitted to one end of this tube. The exhaust pipes were fitted with high pressure, non-return relief valves. When travelling submerged, sea water was used to cool the engine and seepage was removed by a bilge pump.

Maximum diving depth was 15 metres, with three metres of the air tube's 18-metre length available as a safety measure.

The 'submersible tanks' were to be launched from ferries which were hastily made from converted river barges or lighters, though river ferries were also used in the tests. The tanks slid into the water via an elongated ramp made of iron rails. Direction was kept by radio orders from a command vessel to the submerged machines. Underwater navigation was carried out by means of gyro compass and the crew was equipped with submarine-type escape apparatus. The submerged machines were relatively easy to steer as buoyancy partly raised them. When Operation Sea Lion was abandoned, these vehicles were used during the Russian campaign, in 1941, for the crossing of the River Bug.

LAST OF THEIR KIND

The PzKpfw II Ausf D and E were built by Daimler-Benz and were intended to be faster versions of the standard tanks. As far as the turret, superstructure, engine and transmission were concerned they showed no difference from the other Panzer IIs. However, the suspension was completely changed and used four large suspension wheels in Christie tank fashion but with their movement controlled by torsion bars. They could reach 35 mph but their performance across country was considerably slower than that of the standard PzKpfw II.

Because the performance of Models D and E did not come up to expectation they were taken out of service and 95 were converted to a flame-throwing role with the designation *Flammpanzer* II (SdKfz 122). Each was fitted with two projectors covering an arc of 180° each side with a flame range of about 40 yards. This was about the maximum that could be obtained with a pump-fed gun. To obtain greater range it was necessary to use a gas pressure system which introduced problems over stowage. Sufficient fuel was stowed in internal tanks for about 80 shots, each of 2–3 seconds duration.

The hollow charge anti-tank missile had by 1940 become a menace to be reckoned with and then it was decided that all future AFVs were to be up-armoured by the addition of spaced plates to reduce the effect of the new missiles. Thus, when the last of the Panzer II series, the PzKpfw II Ausf F, appeared in late 1940 it carried this 'spaced armour' feature.

The vehicle weighed 9½ tons with 35 mm of armour on the front and 20 mm on the sides. Otherwise it was exactly the same as the PzKpfw II Ausf C in appearance with engine, transmission, armament and suspension remaining unchanged. The top speed was considerably reduced but this was a penalty that had been foreseen when the order authorising additional armour was issued. Crew losses had been heavy enough to justify the reduction in performance in the hope of saving lives. Production of the Model F was to have been at the rate of 45 per month but rarely reached this target.

In 1941 a new specification was issued which called for a ten-ton vehicle with more armour than the Model F and a higher speed. To meet this requirement MAN delivered a chassis in September which had a Maybach HL-P engine developing 200 hp and was capable of a top speed of 40 mph. The tank was to have had 30 mm of armour, a three-man crew, and was to have been armed with a 20-mm type 38 gun of higher velocity than that used in the other models, together with a 7·92-mm machine-gun. Production was scheduled for July 1942 but by then the PzKpfw II was so obviously obsolete in its tank role that the order was cancelled.

Prototype for the Lynx

The prototype of the PzKpfw II Ausf L (Sdkfz 123) *Luchs* (Lynx) (VK 1303) appeared in mild steel in 1942, but its development story goes back to 1938 when Daimler-Benz were given instructions to produce a new version of PzKpfw II 'with principal emphasis on increased speed' under the development number VK 901. A Maybach HL 45 six-cylinder petrol engine was used which gave 145 hp and a top speed for the tank of 32 mph. The specified speed was 37·5 mph but that was difficult to achieve because no engine of the necessary power (200 hp) was available at the time. VK 901 had 30 mm of front armour and weighed 9·2 tons. It was armed with a 20-mm KwK 38 tank gun and a 7·92-mm machine-gun which was mounted coaxially; both guns were installed in a stabilised mounting.

The manufacture of 75 pre-production machines began in 1940. The third prototype VK 903 had a turret from VK 1303 which became the Lynx and which had been equipped with a range finder and locating instruments. This substitution of turrets gives some idea of the complexity of the German tank programme, for at that time the Lynx chassis had been built by MAN. The interplay of one model on another is difficult to disentangle, but development was on a most extensive scale possibly because of Hitler's continued interest in all sorts of new projects.

To complicate matters even further, Daimler-Benz and MAN together received another contract in December 1939 for a very different type of machine. VK 1601 was to carry 'the thickest possible armour' with a crew of three men. The Maybach III 45 engine of 200 hp was used for the project giving a top speed of 20 mph with an all-up weight of 16½ tons. Frontal armour was 80 mm thick and the side armour was 50 mm. Armament was the 20-mm KwK 38 gun and a machine-gun in a stabilised mount.

Both VK 901 and VK 1601 used a new type of suspension with five large overlapping suspension wheels and no return rollers. Torsion bar springing was used. This type of suspension, which had already been tried out on VK 601 (the PzKpfw I prototype of the 6-ton tank) ultimately led to the Panther and Tiger suspension where overlapping became interleaving, a necessary step to reduce ground pressure but one

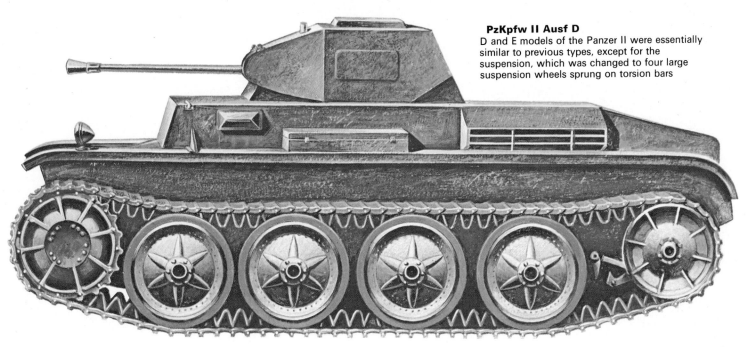

PzKpfw II Ausf D
D and E models of the Panzer II were essentially similar to previous types, except for the suspension, which was changed to four large suspension wheels sprung on torsion bars

which brought its own problems, mainly track jamming.

Out of these two models VK 1301, *Luchs*, was born. VK 901 was considered too light for its proposed role and VK 1601 was much too heavy. The prototype VK 1301 in mild steel ran in April 1942, looking very like VK 901. Various alterations were made to this first prototype and VK 1303, the third prototype, was accepted for production at a weight of 11·8 tons, a reduction of a little over a ton on the first prototype VK 1301.

Different designations

Intended primarily for reconnaissance the Lynx was also given the designation *Panzerspähwagen* II (20-mm KwK 38) *Luchs* with the same Ordnance number, SdKfz 123. It weighed 11·8 tons, had a crew of four men, and was fitted with a Maybach III 66P six-cylinder engine which developed 180 hp. The drive was taken to the front sprocket through a six-speed syncromesh gear box and controlled differential steering on the cross shafts. The maximum speed was 38 mph. The Lynx used the same five overlapping suspension wheel suspension that had been developed on VK901 and VK 1601 with torsion bar springing. Frontal armour was 30 mm and the side plates 20 mm. MAN built the chassis and Daimler-Benz the hulls and turrets. One hundred of these tanks were fitted with 20-mm guns and a further 31 were fitted with 50-mm KwK 39 L/60 guns.

In 1941 the Army Weapons Branch called for a vehicle capable of undertaking battle reconnaissance, in contrast to the Lynx which was intended for general reconnaissance and was not intended to take part in the main battle. The new contract given to MAN and Daimler-Benz was for VK 1602 (inspired by VK 1601) which has already been mentioned as one of the forerunners of the Lynx.

The new tank, Leopard, was to have 80 mm of armour on the turret and the front and 60 mm on the sides. It was to have a 550 hp engine to give it a top speed of 37 mph and it was to be armed with a 50-mm type 39 L/60 gun and a machine-gun coaxially mounted. It was to have a crew of four men, but the tank never went into production although the turrets were used for the famous eight-wheeled armoured car, the Puma.

The last light tanks

Aside from several minor experimental versions of the Panzer I (including a proposed heavily armoured Ausf C), the Lynx and the Leopard represented the final German efforts at light tank production. Like the other combatants in the Second World War, the Germans discovered only too quickly that the light tank's recce function could be fulfilled just as easily by armoured cars – but in the Wehrmacht at least the Panzer I and II hulls soldiered on until 1945 as the basic chassis for numerous self-propelled guns, as driver trainers, or as munitions carriers.

A PzKpfw II Ausf B passes an abandoned Russian BT-7A. Soviet tank losses in the opening phases of Barbarossa were immense, and by December 1941 over 15,000 machines had been destroyed

PzKpfw II Ausf F
Basically similar to Ausf C, with spaced armour plates added in an attempt to reduce crew losses. An extra 35 mm of armour on the front and 20 mm on sides increased its weight to 9·5 tons, with a consequent loss of performance

Panzer II Suspension Development
Top row: Two examples of sprung girder types derived from British Carden-Loyd types and used on pre-production machines. Bottom left: Leaf Spring (Ausf A, B and C). Right: Christie type (Ausf D and E)

Bundesarchiv

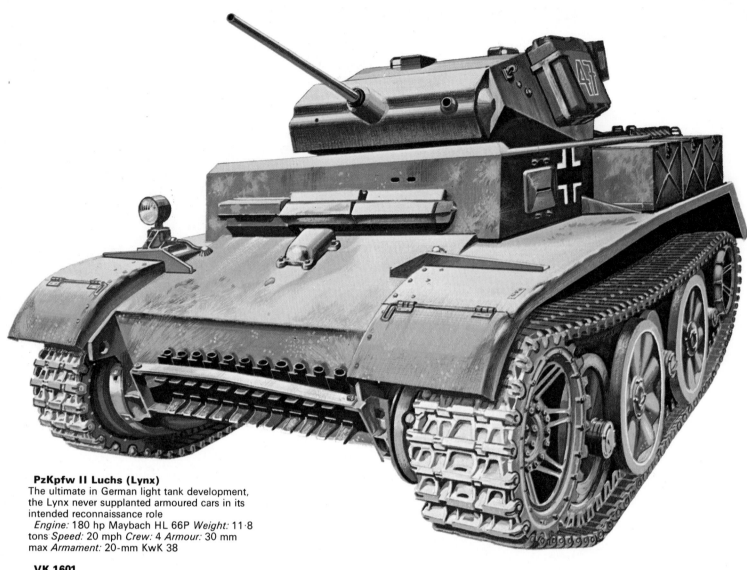

PzKpfw II Luchs (Lynx)
The ultimate in German light tank development, the Lynx never supplanted armoured cars in its intended reconnaissance role
Engine: 180 hp Maybach HL 66P *Weight:* 11·8 tons *Speed:* 20 mph *Crew:* 4 *Armour:* 30 mm max *Armament:* 20-mm KwK 38

VK 1601
A 1939 prototype for a heavily armoured reconnaissance tank, VK 1601 proved much too heavy, though its suspension was later used in the Lynx light tank
Engine: 200 hp Maybach HL 45 *Weight:* 16·5 tons *Speed:* 20 mph *Crew:* 3 *Armour:* 80 mm max *Armament:* 20-mm KwK 38; 1 mg

THE TIDE TURNS

German tanks had overrun mainland Europe and half of Western Russia – but a bitter lesson waited in the snows of Russia and the response of Allied designers to the German challenge. Before the second generation of tanks appeared, the older models would have to stem the tide . . .

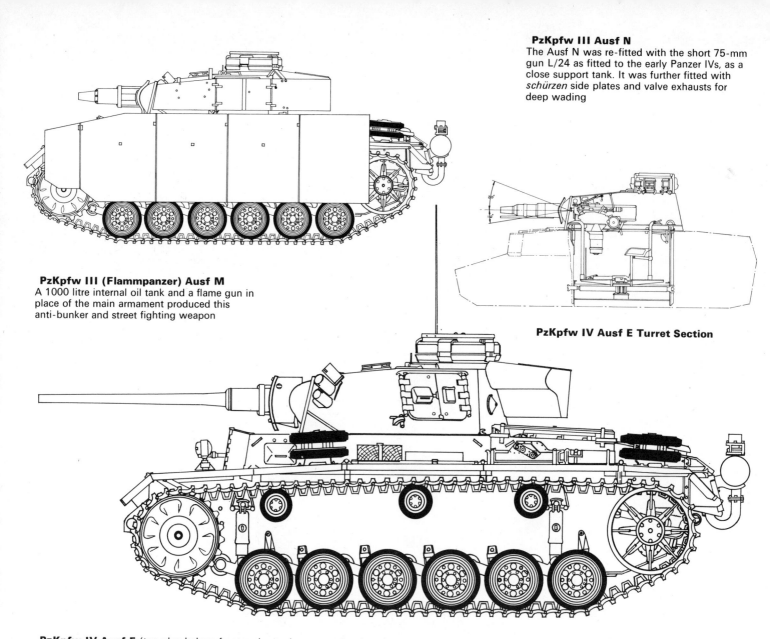

PzKpfw III Ausf N
The Ausf N was re-fitted with the short 75-mm gun L/24 as fitted to the early Panzer IVs, as a close support tank. It was further fitted with *schürzen* side plates and valve exhausts for deep wading

PzKpfw III (Flammpanzer) Ausf M
A 1000 litre internal oil tank and a flame gun in place of the main armament produced this anti-bunker and street fighting weapon

PzKpfw IV Ausf E Turret Section

PzKpfw IV Ausf E (top plan below, front and rear views opposite above)
Ausf E showed several modifications over the Ausf D – the commander's cupola was moved forward, armour improved and several details changed. Production began in 1939, making it available for the invasion of France

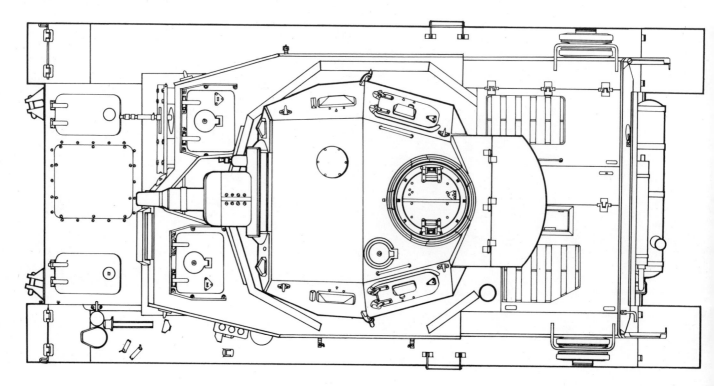

From late 1941 onwards, there was a great change in German fortune as far as tank warfare was concerned. First of all, the Soviet T-34 tank appeared on the Russian Front and caused a fundamental re-appraisal of tank production and a concentration on new designs – though in truth there was no lack of designs in the pipeline at this time. Secondly, in the early part of 1942 the new American-built medium tanks appeared in the Western Desert. First came the M3 medium tanks (Grant and Lee) at the Battle of Gazala in May 1942, then the much superior M4 medium tank (Sherman) reached service for the Battle of Alamein in October 1942.

Both these American vehicles gave Allied tank men, for the first time, a tank with a 75-mm gun which matched the contemporary German weapons, could fire HE and AP ammunition, and was suitable for mass-production. The Sherman was big enough for future development, too, and

by 1944 had been up-gunned to take a 17-pounder high velocity gun (the British Sherman Firefly) or the 76-mm gun (the American 'Easy Eight' model). There was an associated programme of American tank destroyers, too, with 90-mm guns, and overwhelming Allied air superiority on all fronts – not to mention the big Russian Stalin tanks and the American Pershings which were in service in the last year of the war.

On the defensive

All these factors combined to put German AFVs and tactics into a defensive rather than an offensive situation. The Panzer III was soon outmoded, for the 50-mm gun was the biggest it could carry. The Ausf M was a refined version of the Ausf L, with the side escape doors eliminated to simplify production. Last of the line was the Ausf N which, ironically, took over the Panzer IV's intended role as a 'support' tank. It

was fitted with the short low velocity 75-mm KwK L/24 from the early marks of PzKpfw IV, and production of the PzKpfw III as a gun tank ceased completely in August 1943. However, the vehicle soldiered on in service in less important areas until the war's end, was used for training, and was converted to special purpose use. In addition the Panzer III chassis was used for a whole range of assault gun and tank destroyer conversions which played an important part in the Panzer Divisions until the end of the war.

The Panzer IV, being a bigger vehicle, took over the Panzer III's envisaged role of principal battle tank and was truthfully described as the 'workhorse of the Panzer Divisions'. Though inferior in shape and equipment to the T-34 and the post-1942 German designs, the Panzer IV had the virtues of the Sherman – it was reliable and relatively simple to maintain. The PzKpfw IV Ausf E was a major production type with

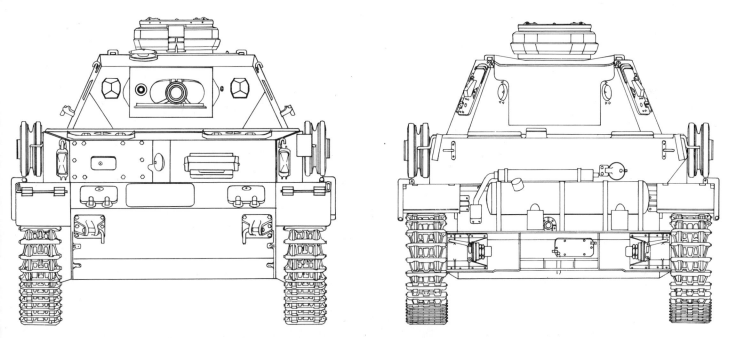

PzKpfw IV Ausf E in a column of armour, clearly showing the additional armour plates

Bundesarchiv

a simplified one-piece front to the super-structure, and retained the 75-mm gun. The Ausf F (later re-designated Ausf F1) was an up-armoured model with basic armour of 50 mm at the front and a ball-mounted hull machine-gun. Like the later models of the Panzer III it had a simplified idler wheel and widened tracks.

The major development, however, was the PzKpfw IV Ausf F2, the original F re-armed with a long high velocity 75-mm gun, and produced specifically to restore the balance of fire-power to the Afrika Korps in 1942 when the American-built tanks with 75-mm guns appeared. This vehicle – known to the British troops as the

'Mk IV Special' – was exceptionally effective, but Rommel could never get enough of them to restore the Panzer Divisions of the Afrika Korps to their original dominating position on the battlefield. The PzKpfw IV Ausf G was a similar vehicle, but built from the start with the high velocity gun, and with an improved up-armoured turret and detail changes.

Improved armament

The new gun, KwK 40 L/43, of the PzKpfw IV Ausf F2 was easily distinguished by its longer barrel and muzzle brake. While the first production model was fitted with a single-baffle globular muzzle brake, later

vehicles had a double brake. The gun itself was capable of penetrating homogenous armour of 77 mm thickness at 2000 yards using PzGr 39 at normal impact. It could fire at least six different kinds of ammunition and 87 rounds were carried, plus 2250 rounds of 7·92-mm ammunition for the two MG 34 machine-guns. One of these was mounted co-axially on the right side of the gun; the other was ball-mounted on the right side of the front vertical plate and worked by the radio-operator. Turret traverse was effected by either hand or electric power supplied from a generator, driven by a DKW two-cylinder two-cycle 10 hp 500 cc petrol engine.

PzKpfw IV Ausf F2 Turret and Hull Front
The long barrelled 75-mm KwK L/43 with single-baffle globular muzzle brake made this mark of the Panzer IV easy to distinguish. The vision ports on the turret sides, and the loader's on the turret front, were omitted

PzKpfw IV Ausf F
The Ausf F (or F1) appeared in 1940, and had profited from the experience of the Polish campaign. Armour was increased, track widened and visibility improved, though its armament was still not equal to the T-34's
Engine: 265 hp Maybach HL 120 *Weight:* 22 tons *Speed:* 25 mph
Crew: 5 *Armour:* 50 mm max *Armament:* short 75-mm; 2 mg

By mid-1943, the vehicle had been further refined with the appearance of the PzKpfw IV Ausf H. Similar to the G model, it had a still more powerful 75-mm gun, the L/48, which was about 15 in longer than the L/43. A new cupola with 100-mm armour was fitted, and some vehicles had 30-mm plates of extra armour welded or bolted on the nose. Later vehicles were built new with 85 mm thick frontal armour. Simplified suspension components were used to reduce production costs. For protection from hollow charge anti-tank projectiles of the bazooka type, mild steel skirt armour plates were suspended from rails attached to the superstructure, since hollow charge

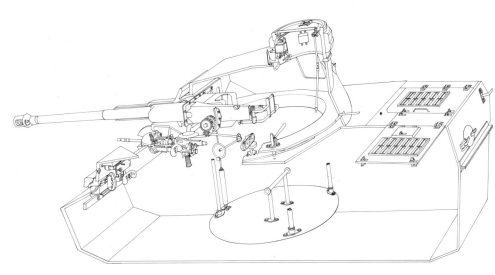

PzKpfw IV Ausf F2 Interior Detail
Showing turret and fighting compartment, driver's and machine-gunner/radio-operator's hull positions. The long 75-mm gun still left plenty of room in the turret cage

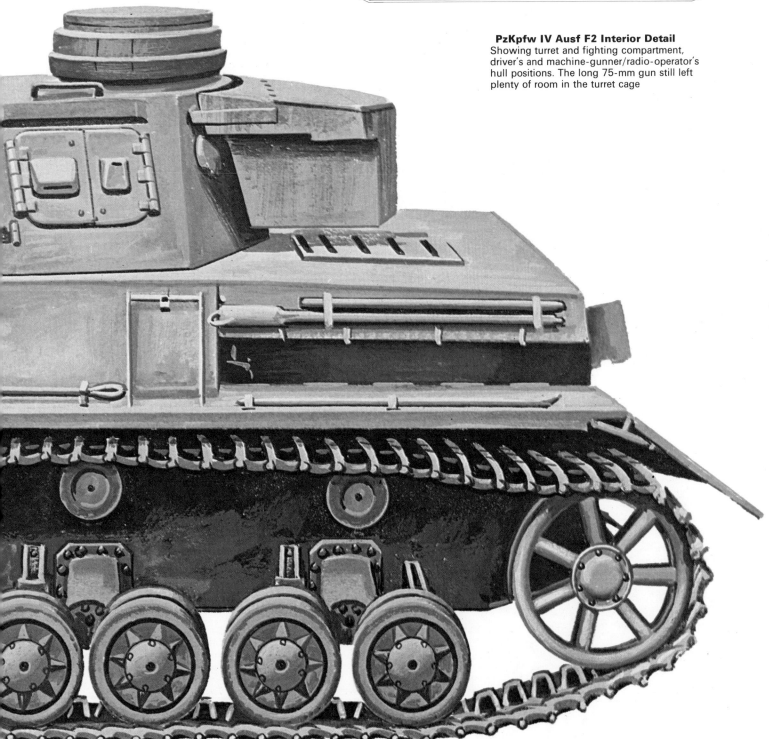

weapons were now in Allied service on an increasing scale. Zimmerit anti-magnetic compound also made its appearance at this time to prevent magnetic charges being placed on the vehicle.

Last of the PzKpfw IV line was the Ausf J, with further changes to simplify production: the generator which provided power traverse for the turret was removed and replaced by extra fuel tanks. Heavy gauge mesh wire replaced the steel skirt armour, and most late vehicles had spaced armour plates right round the turret. Appearing in mid-1944, the Ausf J remained in production until the end of the war.

In 1942, an early attempt at rationalisation was the PzKpfw III/IV, combining parts from both tanks to make a standard battle tank using a Famo-type suspension similar to that fitted to the German half-tracks. However, the obvious limitations of the vehicle's development potential led to the hybrid III/IV model being dropped as a project, and work concentrated on the big Tiger tank.

The PzKpfw IV Ausf F1 retained the short 75-mm gun, and was quickly replaced by the Ausf F2

Bundesarchiv

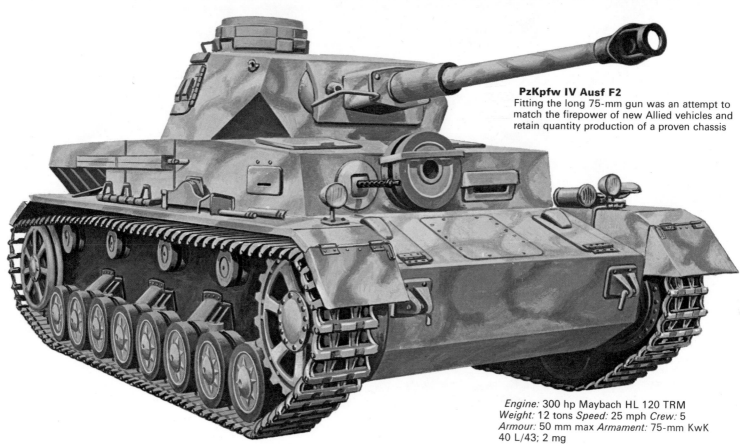

PzKpfw IV Ausf F2
Fitting the long 75-mm gun was an attempt to match the firepower of new Allied vehicles and retain quantity production of a proven chassis

Engine: 300 hp Maybach HL 120 TRM
Weight: 12 tons *Speed:* 25 mph *Crew:* 5
Armour: 50 mm max *Armament:* 75-mm KwK 40 L/43; 2 mg

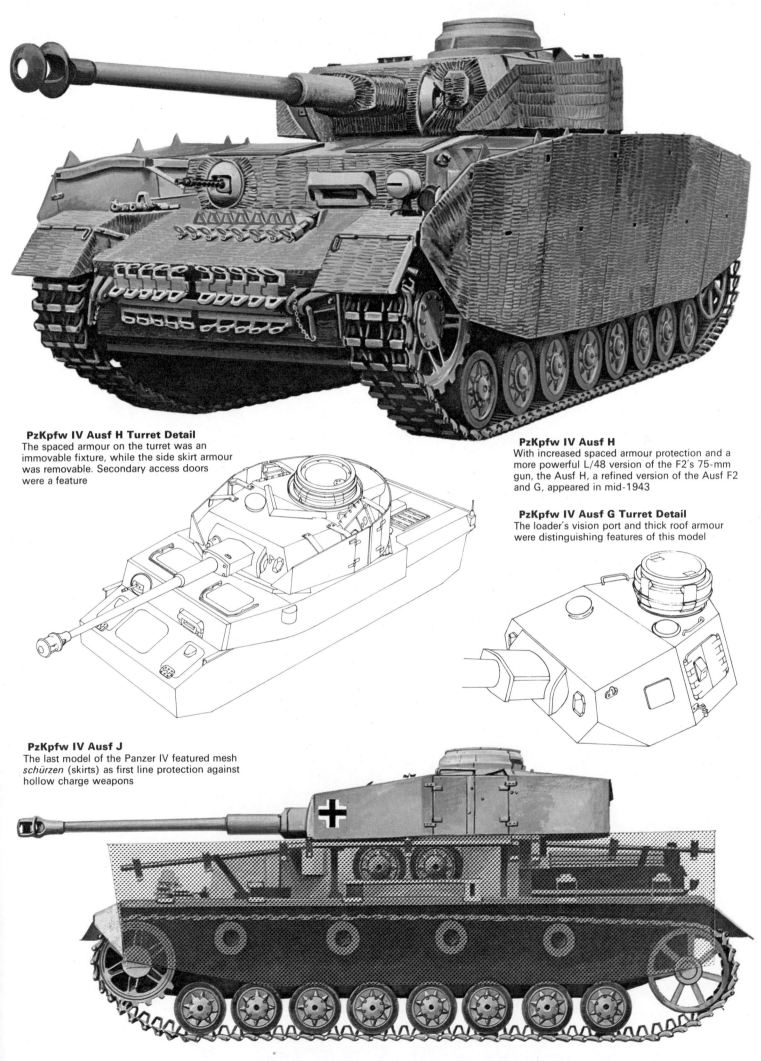

PzKpfw IV Ausf H Turret Detail
The spaced armour on the turret was an immovable fixture, while the side skirt armour was removable. Secondary access doors were a feature

PzKpfw IV Ausf H
With increased spaced armour protection and a more powerful L/48 version of the F2's 75-mm gun, the Ausf H, a refined version of the Ausf F2 and G, appeared in mid-1943

PzKpfw IV Ausf G Turret Detail
The loader's vision port and thick roof armour were distinguishing features of this model

PzKpfw IV Ausf J
The last model of the Panzer IV featured mesh *schürzen* (skirts) as first line protection against hollow charge weapons

A NEW BREED OF PANZER

The Tiger tank originated from development started in 1937. Henschel were instructed to design and construct a 30- to 33-ton tank prototype as a possible successor to the Panzer IV. The new vehicle was known as the DW I, DW being an abbreviation of *Durchbrüchswagen* (breakthrough vehicle). However, after one chassis with interleaved road wheel suspension had been built and testing had commenced, the trials were suspended in 1938 to allow work to be carried out on a further design for a 65-ton tank, the VK 6501. The VK 6501 was itself a further development of the original Panzer VI (the NbFz Model B).

Two prototypes of the VK 6501 were built and were undergoing trials when the project was cancelled and development resumed on the DW I. By 1940 Henschel had so improved the original design that it was re-designated DW 2. In this form it weighed 32 tons and accommodated a crew of five. The planned armament was the short 75-mm gun with two MG 34 machine-guns. Trials were carried out with a prototype chassis until 1941, by which time Henschel had received an order for a new design in the same class and weight as the DW 2. The development designation for the new vehicle was VK 3001, and Henschel's competitors, Porsche, MAN and Daimler-Benz, were also invited to submit designs.

The Henschel version, VK 3001 (H), was a development of the DW 2 and four prototypes were built, two in March 1941 and two the following October, differing only in detail from each other. The superstructure of the VK 3001 (H) resembled that of the Panzer IV, and the suspension consisted of seven interleaved road wheels and three return rollers per side. It was planned to mount the 75-mm L/48 gun in this vehicle, but the appearance that year of the Russian T-34 with its 76-mm gun, rendered the vehicle obsolete and development was discontinued. Two of the VK 3001 (H) chassis were converted to self-propelled guns, by lengthening and mounting a 128-mm K 40 gun. These two vehicles were used in Russia in 1942.

Prototypes from Porsche
The Porsche version, VK 3001 (P), was also known to its designers as the Leopard or Type 100. This turretless prototype incorporated several new design features such as petrol-electric drive and longitudinal torsion bar suspension. MAN and Daimler-Benz also constructed prototypes to this design but like the Henschel project they had become obsolete.

With the order for the VK 3001 an additional order had also been placed for a 36-ton tank under the designation VK 3601. This specification had been personally proposed by Hitler, and included a powerful, high velocity gun, heavy armour and a maximum speed of at least 25° mph. A prototype of this project was built by Henschel in March 1942, but experimental work on both the VK 3001 and VK 3601 was stopped when a further order for a 45-ton tank was received in May 1941.

Designated VK 4501, the intended vehicle was to mount a tank version of the 88-mm gun. With the order came a stipulation that the prototype was to be ready in time for Hitler's birthday on 20 April 1942, when a full demonstration of its capabilities was to be staged. As design time was limited Henschel decided to incorporate the best features of their VK 3001 (H) and VK 3601

(H) projects into a vehicle of the weight and class required. They planned to build two models, the type H 1 mounting an 88-mm KwK 36 L/56 gun, and the Type H 2 with a 75-mm KwK L/70, although the H 2 existed only as a wooden mock-up at that time.

Porsche also received an order for a prototype to the VK 4501 specification and like Henschel they decided to incorporate as many as possible of the design features from their previous model, the VK 3001 (P), which had performed well on trials.

The demonstration of the two competing prototypes, the VK 4501 (H) and VK 4501 (P) duly took place before Hitler at Rastenburg, when the Henschel design was considered to be superior. An order for production to commence in August 1942, was given and the vehicle was designated *Panzerkampfwagen VI Tiger* (Tiger) Ausf E. The Ordnance Dept. number was SdKfz 181.

Production history
The Tiger was subsequently in production for two years, from August 1942 until August 1944, and in this period a total of 1350 vehicles were delivered out of 1376 ordered. Maximum monthly production was achieved in April 1944, when 104 Tigers were built. It is interesting to note that the specified weight of 45 tons was exceeded in production by about 11 tons.

The Tiger was technically the most sophisticated and best engineered vehicle of its time. The hull was divided into four compartments: the forward two housed the driver and hull gunner/radio operator, the centre was the fighting compartment, and the engine compartment was at the rear. The driver sat on the left and steered by means of a wheel which acted hydraulically on the Tiger's controlled differential steering unit. Emergency steering was provided for by two steering levers one either side of the driver operating disc brakes. These brakes were also used for vehicle parking and were connected to a foot pedal and parking brake lever. A visor was provided for the driver and this was opened and closed by a sliding shutter worked from a hand wheel on the front vertical plate.

Fixed episcopes were provided in both the driver's and the wireless operator's escape hatches. A standard German gyro direction indicator and instrument panel were situated to the left and right of the driver's seat respectively. The gearbox separated the two forward crew members' compartments. The machine-gunner/radio-operator seated on the right manned a standard 7·92-mm MG 34 in a ball mounting in the front vertical plate; this was fired by a hand trigger and sighted by a KZF cranked telescope. The radio sets were mounted on a shelf to the operator's left.

The centre fighting compartment was separated from the front compartments by an arched cross member and from the engine compartment in the rear by a solid bulkhead. The floor of the fighting compartment was suspended from the turret by three steel tubes and rotated with the

VK 4501 (P), the Porsche prototype for the Tiger, and Dr Ferdinand Porsche, its designer (in car).
Opposite: A Tiger knocked out by the Americans in Italy

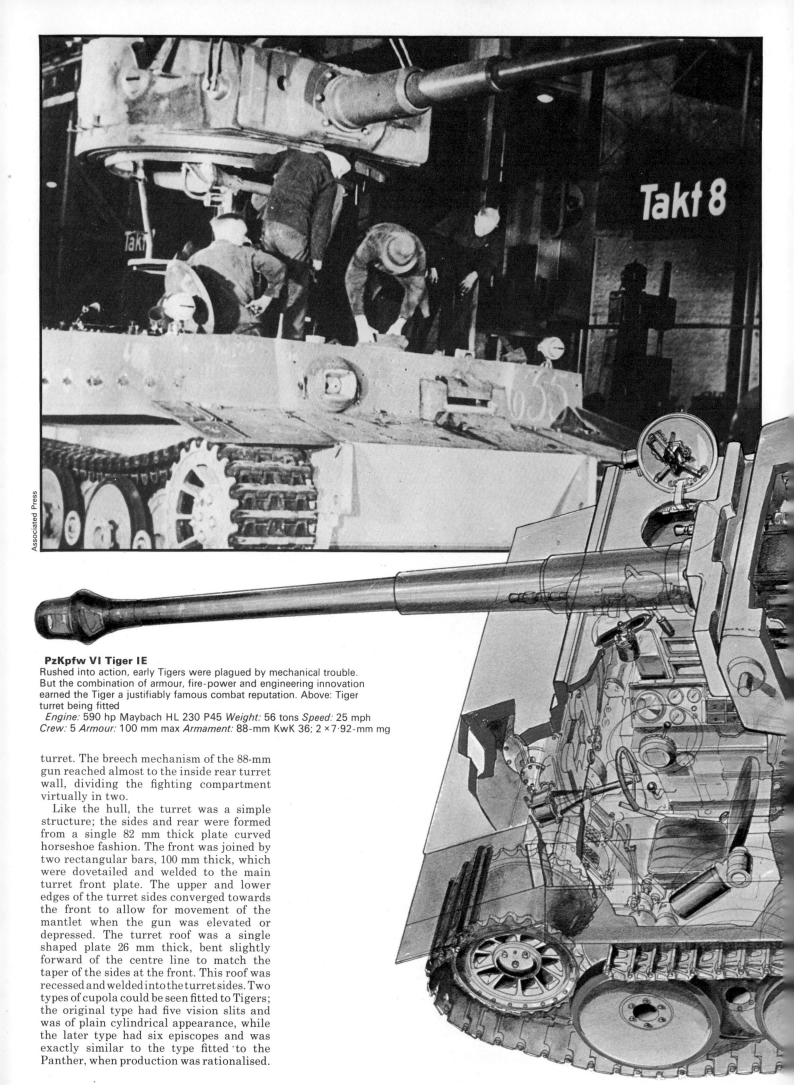

Takt 8

PzKpfw VI Tiger IE
Rushed into action, early Tigers were plagued by mechanical trouble.
But the combination of armour, fire-power and engineering innovation
earned the Tiger a justifiably famous combat reputation. Above: Tiger
turret being fitted
Engine: 590 hp Maybach HL 230 P45 *Weight:* 56 tons *Speed:* 25 mph
Crew: 5 *Armour:* 100 mm max *Armament:* 88-mm KwK 36; 2 × 7·92-mm mg

turret. The breech mechanism of the 88-mm
gun reached almost to the inside rear turret
wall, dividing the fighting compartment
virtually in two.

Like the hull, the turret was a simple
structure; the sides and rear were formed
from a single 82 mm thick plate curved
horseshoe fashion. The front was joined by
two rectangular bars, 100 mm thick, which
were dovetailed and welded to the main
turret front plate. The upper and lower
edges of the turret sides converged towards
the front to allow for movement of the
mantlet when the gun was elevated or
depressed. The turret roof was a single
shaped plate 26 mm thick, bent slightly
forward of the centre line to match the
taper of the sides at the front. This roof was
recessed and welded into the turret sides. Two
types of cupola could be seen fitted to Tigers;
the original type had five vision slits and
was of plain cylindrical appearance, while
the later type had six episcopes and was
exactly similar to the type fitted to the
Panther, when production was rationalised.

Other external turret fittings were three NbK 39 90-mm smoke generators on either side towards the front, two stowage bins either side towards the front and two stowage bins either side of the centre line at the rear. The bins were used to stow the bedding, rations, packs and other personal effects of the crew.

Tiger I was the first German combat tank to be fitted with overlapping road wheel suspension, arranged with triple overlapping and interleaved wheels of a steel disc type with solid rubber tyres. The overlapping wheel system was adopted for optimum weight distribution. There were eight independently sprung torsion bar axles on each side. In order to carry all the axles inside the hull it was necessary to stagger them on the floor so that the right hand axles trailed aft and the left hand axles led forward. It was thus possible to incorporate the maximum number within the vehicle's length, and this resulted in an

extremely soft and stable ride for a tank of this weight and size.

Two types of track were used: one 28·5 in wide for combat and a narrower one 20·5 in wide for travel and transportation. When the narrow tracks were fitted the outer wheels were removed from each suspension unit. Though this type of suspension gave a superior ride, it also had its drawbacks, one being that the interleaved road wheels were liable to become packed with mud and snow during winter fighting, and if ignored until frozen this could jam the wheels. The Russians discovered this and took advantage of the situation by timing their attacks for dawn, when the vehicles were likely to have become immobilised during the night's frosts.

Very late production Tigers had steel disc type wheels with resilient internal rubber spring rims of the type fitted to the King Tigers and late model Panthers. In Tigers so fitted, the outside run of wheels

was omitted. This obviated to some extent the icing-up problem and also reduced overheating of the axle bearings.

The Tiger was originally fitted with a Maybach V-12 petrol engine, the HL 210 P45 of 21 litres capacity, but it was soon realised that the vehicle was underpowered and an uprated engine, the HL 230 P45 of 24 litres was substituted. The Tigers used in North Africa, and (after early experience of dust) in Russia in summer, were fitted with the Feifel air cleaner system. This was attached to the rear of the hull and linked to the engine over the engine cover plate. These tropical Tigers were known as the Tiger (Tp), but the Feifel air system was soon discontinued to simplify production.

While all earlier designs of German tank had the simple clutch-and-brake type of steering, the Tiger's greatly increased weight necessitated a more refined system. Henschel therefore developed and adopted a special steering unit, similar to the British

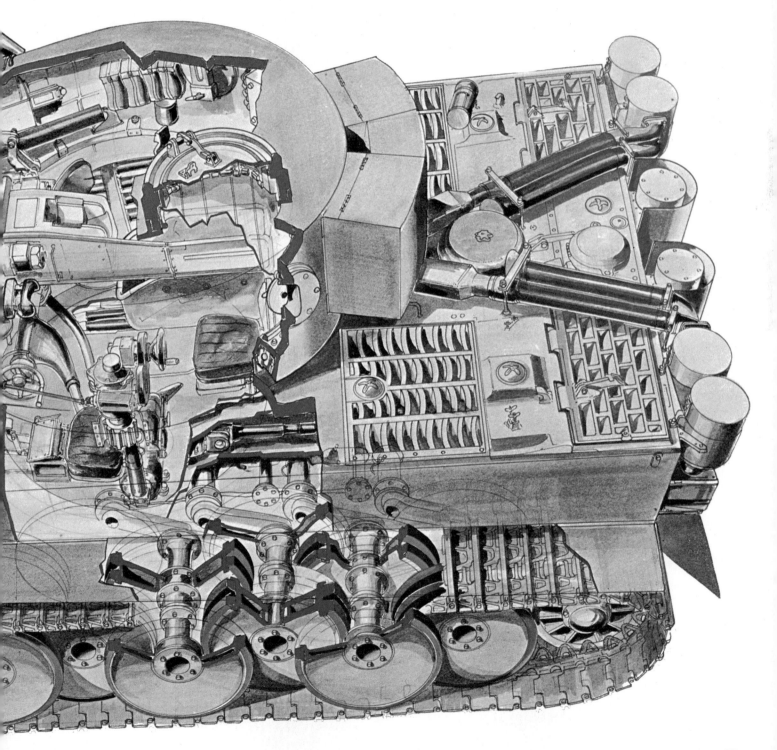

Merritt-Brown type, which was fully regenerative and continuous. It had the added feature of a twin radius turn in each gear. The gearbox, which was based on earlier Maybach types, gave no less than eight forward gear ratios and, with its pre-selector, made the Tiger very light and easy to handle for a vehicle of its size. The Tiger's mechanical layout followed that of previous operational German designs in that the transmission shaft led forward beneath the turret cage to the gearbox set alongside the driver.

The steering unit was mounted transversely in the nose of the tank, a bevel drive leading to a final reduction gear in each front sprocket. Power take-off for the hydraulic turret traverse unit, mounted in the turret floor, was taken from the rear of the gearbox, and it is typical of the Tiger's well-thought out design that the hydraulic unit could be disconnected from the power drive shaft by releasing a dog-clutch, thus allowing the turret to be lifted from the vehicle without the complications of disconnecting any other joints or pipes.

The first production Tigers were elaborately equipped for totally submerged wading to a depth of 13 ft with Snorkel breathing, but this proved an expensive luxury and with the need to simplify production this was discarded. Subsequent Tigers had a wading capability to a maximum depth of 4 ft.

One of the Tiger's biggest advances over any previous design was in its method of construction. In order to simplify assembly as much as possible and allow the use of heavy armour plate, flat sections were used throughout the hull. Hull and superstructure were welded, in contrast to previous German tanks where a bolted joint was used between hull and superstructure. The Tiger front and rear superstructure was in one unit and interlocking stepped joints, secured by welding, were used in the construction of both the lower hull and the superstructure. A pannier was, in effect, formed over each track by extending the superstructure sideways to full width and the complete length of the vehicle was so shaped from front vertical plate to tail plate. The top front plate of the hull covered the full width of the vehicle and it was this extreme width which permitted a turret ring of 6 ft 1 in internal diameter to be fitted which was of ample size to accommodate the breech and mounting of the 88-mm gun. The belly was also in one piece, being a plate 1 in thick and 15 ft $10\frac{1}{4}$ in long by 5 ft 11 in wide.

High velocity gun

The 88-mm KwK 36 gun which formed the Tiger's main armament had ballistic characteristics similar to those of the famous Flak 18 and Flak 36 88-mm high velocity AA guns from which it was derived. The principal modifications were the addition of a muzzle brake and electric firing by a trigger-operated primer on the elevating handwheel. A 7·92-mm MG 34 was coaxially mounted in the left side of the mantlet and was fired by mechanical linkage from a foot pedal operated by the gunner. The 88-mm had a breech of the semi-automatic falling wedge type scaled up from the conventional type used on smaller German tank guns. The weight of the barrel was balanced by a large coil spring housed in a cylinder on the left hand front of the turret. Elevation and hand traverse were controlled by handwheels to the right and left of the gunner respectively

and an additional traverse handwheel was provided for the commander's use in an emergency.

The hydraulic power traverse was controlled by a rocking footplate operated by the gunner's right foot. Because of the turret's weight, traverse was necessarily low-geared both in hand and power. It took 720 turns of the gunner's handwheel, for instance, to move the turret through 360° and power traverse through any large arc demanded a good deal of footwork (and concentration) by the gunner. Allied tanks – always more lightly armoured – were often able to take advantage of this limitation to get in the first shot when surprising a Tiger from the side or rear. In fact, this became almost standard procedure for engaging a Tiger tank, one tank attracting its attention from the front while one or two others attempted to work round to the flanks or rear to get in a shot at the more vulnerable areas of the vehicle.

For sighting purposes the gunner was provided with a binocular telescope, a clinometer for use in HE shoots, and a turret position indicator dial. Ammunition for the 88-mm gun was stowed partly in bins each side of the fighting compartment and partly alongside the driver and under the turret floor.

Early production Tigers were fitted with 'S' mine dischargers on top of the superstructure, a total of five being mounted in various positions on the front, sides and rear. These devices were installed for protection against infantry attacking with such anti-tank weapons as magnetic mines or pole charges. The 'S' mine was an anti-personnel bomb shaped like a jam jar and was about 5 in deep by 4 in wide. It was shot some 3 to 5 ft into the air, where it was set to explode and scatter its contents – 360 $\frac{3}{8}$-in diameter steel balls.

However, when the turret design was amended in late 1943 to incorporate a periscope of the type fitted to the Panther, a standard *Nahverteidigungswaffe* (close-in defence weapon) was fitted in the turret roof in place of the extractor fan, which was itself moved to the centre. The *Nahverteidgungswaffe* had all-round traverse and was internally loaded, rendering the somewhat awkward S mine dischargers superfluous.

There were two Tiger tank variants: Tiger Command Tank (*Panzerbefehlswagen*), was designated PzBefWg *Tiger* Ausf E, SdKfz 267 or 258. The difference between these two sub-variants was solely in the wireless equipment fitted, the SdKfz 267 carrying combinations of the Fu 5 and Fu 8 radio and

Tiger Stowage
Below: Fighting compartment and turret, side view (left) rear view (right). Centre: Driver's compartment (left), hull gunner's compartment (right). Bottom: Tiger I side section

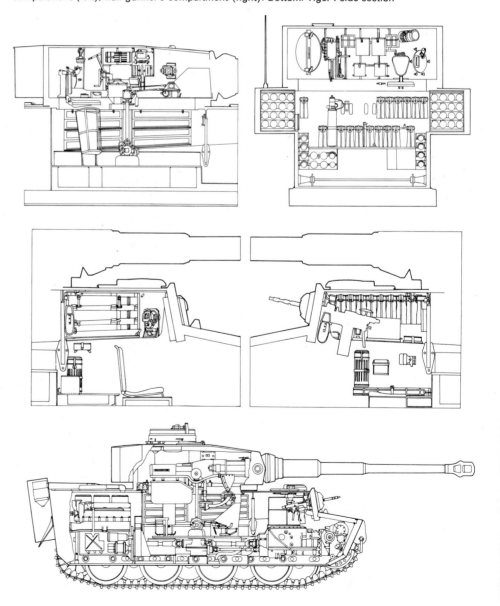

An early production model Tiger Ausf E, a disturbing sight in a French farmyard in 1944

Bundesarchiv

the SdKfz 268 being fitted with combinations of the Fu 5 and Fu 7.

In addition there was the Tiger Armoured Recovery Vehicle, designated *Bergepanzer Tiger* I Ausf E. This was no more than a towing vehicle for assisting crippled or otherwise malfunctioning Tigers back to an area where repairs could be effected. The adaptation involved the removal of the main armament, sealing of the mantlet, fixing the turret in the traversed position and fitting a winch to the turret rear with a wire rope guide on the front. No lifting gear was provided.

At the time of its debut in service in late 1942, the PzKpfw VI Tiger I was an outstanding design among its contemporaries by virtue of its powerful gun and armour protection of up to 100 mm thick. These factors made the 56-ton Tiger the most formidable fighting vehicle then in service. It was, however, relatively costly to produce in terms of man-hours and difficult to adapt for mass production. In January 1944, the heavier and generally superior Tiger II Ausf B went into production with the result that successively fewer E models were produced until they were finally phased out of production completely in August 1944.

It was intended to use the Tiger as a heavy infantry or assault gun, and Tiger battalions were organised as independent units under GHQ troops. Armoured divisions engaged in a major operation would receive an allotment of Tigers to spearhead an attack, but owing to the Tiger's basic lack of manoeuvrability, it was always considered necessary to employ lighter tanks in supporting platoons on the flanks. Normally Panzer IIIs or IVs fulfilled this function.

It was later decided to include Tigers in the basic organisation of armoured divisions, but due to attrition which depleted the number of Tigers serviceable at any one time, it was never possible to put this plan into operation except in Waffen-SS armoured divisions. These divisions were among the first to receive Tigers, which went into service with such famous formations as the I SS Panzer Division *Leibstandarte* SS 'Adolf Hitler', and the II SS Panzer Division

'Das Reich'. The fact that there were never sufficient Tigers to go round was probably the greatest comfort that opposing forces could take from their appearance.

However, the Tiger's debut was not very sensational. Hitler was impatient to make use of the formidable new weapon as soon as possible in September 1942, against the opinion of senior staff officers who favoured building up Tiger strength during the winter, and perfecting tactics and training for a mass Tiger offensive in Russia in the Spring of 1943.

Therefore, in the earliest Tiger action of the war, on 23 September 1942, near Leningrad, the employment of this sinister-looking vehicle was restricted to such limited numbers that resolute action by anti-tank gunners taking full advantage of the situation was more than enough to counter their impact. This attack took place on terrain unsuitable for any successful tank action, and, restricted to single-file progress on forest tracks through swamps, the Tigers proved to be an easy target for the Soviet gunners posted to cover the tracks.

The British first encountered the Tiger in February 1943, near Pont du Fahs in Tunisia. Having received advance warning of the impending attack, the British anti-tank gunners were concealed with their 6-pounders with instructions to hold their fire until signalled. Two Tigers, flanked by nine Panzer IIIs and Panzer IVs, advanced with artillery support and were not engaged until the range had closed to 500 yards on each flank. Fire from the 6-pounders knocked out both Tigers.

Defensive role

Although the Tiger had been conceived as a powerful assault weapon, the changing tide of war in 1943/44 meant that Tigers were more and more used in a defensive role, in which they were very successful. The Tiger's bulk, limited mobility and susceptibility to mechanical failure were severe disadvantages in a war of movement. The limitations of very large, heavily armoured tanks were well demonstrated by the Tiger, but the conclusions were too late to influence the new generations of heavy AFVs which were to appear in 1944/45.

The story of Henschel's Tiger is inextricably tied up with the close rival designs of

Porsche, which were produced to meet the same *Heereswaffenamt* specification. The first Porsche design was to meet the same VK 3001 requirement as the first Henschel prototype. Strictly speaking this nominal 30-tonner was a replacement design for the Panzer IV and not a 'heavy tank' in the later sense of the term.

The Porsche design, known to the Army as the VK 3001 (P) was designated the Type 100 Leopard by the factory, and two prototypes were built in 1940. Porsche used a hull similar in shape to that of the existing Panzer IV, but employed petrol-electric drive with two air-cooled motors powering electric motors driving the front sprockets. Steering and gear changing was also electric, and there was torsion bar suspension. On test the vehicle put up a good running performance.

In May 1941, Porsche received the same development contract for the VK 4501 requirement, calling for a 45-ton vehicle mounting an 88-mm gun and to be ready for production within one year. The prototype was to be ready (with Henschel's prototype) for demonstration before Hitler in April 1942. With time running out, Porsche utilised the same sort of drive arrangement that had been developed for the now-abandoned VK 3001 (P). The new design was designated Type 101 by Porsche and featured petrol-electric drive as before. The petrol engines were air-cooled and proved a constant source of trouble in the design. Porsche contemplated hydraulic transmission as an alternative to electric transmission.

As a result of the competitive trials, however, the conventionally driven Henschel design was preferred to Porsche's, and the main production contract for what eventually became known as the Tiger went to Henschel. Only a few pilot models of the Porsche design were actually completed as gun tanks, and these were designated PzKpfw VI VK 4501 (P), Tiger (P), to distinguish them from the Henschel Tiger.

The only portion of the Porsche Tiger to enter production was the turret. This was designed by Krupp with the adapted L/56 gun. Henschel had contemplated a turret with a tapered-bore gun firing hard tungsten-steel armour-piercing shells. The scarcity of tungsten and the difficulties of machining the gun barrel led to the abandonment of this idea at an early stage, and the simple turret with conventional 88-mm gun intended for the Porsche was put into production for the Henschel Tiger.

Ninety Porsche Tigers had been ordered, however, partly as a safeguard against delays or failure of the Henschel Tiger and partly to appease Porsche and, in turn, Hitler, who admired Porsche's technical brilliance. But the mechanically unreliable Porsche Tigers were not wanted by the Army, and there remained the problem of how to utilise the redundant chassis. It was decided eventually to convert them to *Panzerjäger* (heavy tank destroyers) and in late 1942, 85 of the completed chassis were transferred from the Steyr-Daimler factory at Nibelungen (the builders of Porsche designs) to Alkett for completion in their new form. Dr Porsche supervised the design of the new vehicle, which was subsequently designated *Jagdpanzer Ferdinand* (after Porsche's first name) and later *Panzerjäger Tiger* (P) *Elefant* (SdKfz 184). These vehicles made their battle debut – unsuccessfully as it turned out – in the great Kursk tank battle.

THE PANTHER
THE
EQUALISER

The unexpected appearance of the revolutionary T-34 tank in Soviet hands rendered all existing German front line tanks obsolete almost literally overnight and there was no tank of comparable size or performance available to the Germans, who did not until then suspect the Russians of having anything of such advanced design. This complacency had been caused entirely by the excellence and versatility of the Panzer IV, even though work on a planned successor had started in 1937. By 1941 the prototypes by Henschel, VK 3001 (H), and Porsche, VK 3001 (P), had been completed but, just prior to the invasion of Russia, when the T-34 was met, requirements were changed yet again in favour of a larger design with an 88-mm gun in the 45-ton class, the VK 4501. This eventually became the Tiger heavy tank but because the VK 4501 design was needed urgently, it incorporated many features from the earlier development prototypes and the Tiger thus owed nothing to the T-34 design. The 88-mm gun and the heavy (100-mm) armour specified for the VK 4501 design were, however, influenced by the T-34's appearance, for it was considered essential to have a tank with these features in production as a safeguard against any eventual Soviet development of an up-gunned and up-armoured version of the T-34.

Meanwhile General Guderian, by now the commander of *Panzergruppe* II, in whose sector the T-34 was first encountered in large numbers in November 1941, sent a report to his Army Group commander suggesting that the Armaments Ministry should appoint a commission most urgently to investigate what sort of new tank design – and anti-tank gun – would be needed to counter the T-34 threat and restore tank superiority to the Germans. The commission, Guderian suggested, should include representatives of the Army Ordnance Department, the main tank manufacturers, and the tank design section. The Armaments Ministry acted swiftly, and appointed just such a commission which was sent to Guderian's front for an 'on the spot' investigation on 20 November 1941, to assess the key features of the T-34 design.

The three main characteristics of this vehicle which rendered all existing German tanks technically obsolete were: (1) the sloped armour which gave optimum shot deflection all round; (2) the large road wheels which gave a stable and steady ride; and (3) the overhanging gun, a feature previously avoided by the Germans as impracticable. Of these the first was the most revolutionary. Having received the commission's report on 25 November 1941, the Armaments Ministry promptly contracted with two principal armament firms, Daimler-Benz and MAN to produce designs for a new medium tank in the 30- to 35-ton class, under the ordnance designation VK 3002. To be ready the following spring, the specifications called for a vehicle with 60-mm frontal armour and 40-mm side armour, the front and sides to be sloped as in the T-34. A maximum speed of 34 mph was required.

In April 1942 the two designs, VK 3002 (DB) (Daimler-Benz) and VK 3002 (MAN), were submitted to a committee of *Waffenprufamt* 6, the section of the Army Ordnance Department responsible for AFV design and procurement.

Contrasting designs

The designs afforded an interesting contrast. The Daimler-Benz proposal was an almost direct copy of the T-34 in layout, with the addition of a few excellent refinements. It had a hull shape similar to that of the T-34 with turret mounted well forward – so far forward in fact that the driver sat within the turret cage – with remote control hydraulic steering. An MB507 diesel engine was fitted with transmission to the rear sprockets, again exactly duplicating the T-34 layout. Paired steel bogies (without rubber tyres) were suspended by leaf springs, and other features included escape hatches in the hull sides and jettisonable fuel tanks on the hull rear in the T-34 fashion.

The VK 3002 (DB) was in fact a remarkably 'clean' design with much potential. Leaf springs, for example, were cheaper and easier to produce than torsion bars, and the use of all-steel wheels recognised the problem of rubber shortage from the start. The compact engine and transmission at the rear left the fighting compartment unencumbered for future up-gunning or structural change, while the diesel engine itself would have been an advantage in later years when petrol supply became acutely restricted.

By comparison, the VK 3002 (MAN) displayed original German (rather than Russian) thinking: it was sophisticated rather than simple. It had a higher, wider hull than either the VK 3002 (DB) or the T-34, with a large turret placed well back to offset as much as possible the overhang of the long 75-mm gun which was called for as the main armament. Torsion bar suspension was used with interleaved road wheels, while a Maybach HL 210 petrol (gasoline)

V-12 engine was proposed, with drive to the front sprockets. The internal layout followed conventional German practice with stations for the driver and hull gunner/radio-operator in the front compartment.

When the respective Daimler-Benz and MAN designs were submitted by the *Waffenprufamt* 6 committee in April 1942, Hitler was most impressed with the Daimler-Benz T-34 type proposal, though he suggested that the gun be changed from the 75-mm L/48 model to the longer and more powerful L/70 weapon. Hitler's intervention in the proceedings at this stage led to an order for 200 VK 3002 (DB) vehicles being placed, and prototypes actually went into production.

The 'Panther Committee'

However, the committee set up by *Waffenprufamt* 6 – which was already being called unofficially the 'Panther Committee' – preferred the VK 3002 (MAN) design, because it was far more conventional by existing German engineering standards. MAN's proposal was accepted in May 1942 and they were asked to go ahead and produce a mild steel prototype as fast as possible. Later in

Bundesarchiv

1942, the order for the 200 Daimler-Benz vehicles was quietly and discreetly rescinded.

Meanwhile Dipl Ing Kniepkampf, chief engineer and designer of *Waffenprufamt* 6, took personal charge of detail design work on the MAN vehicle. This reflected the priority given to the Panther project. Kniepkampf was a key figure in German AFV design at this time, having been with *Waffenprufamt* 6 since 1936 and remaining as chief engineer almost until the war's end in 1945. Among other things he was principally responsible for German half-track development and introduced many of the characteristic features like interleaved road wheels, torsion bar suspension, and the Maybach-Olvar gearbox to German tanks.

In September 1942 the first pilot model of the VK 3002 (MAN) was completed and tested in the MAN factory grounds at Nuremberg. This was closely followed by the second pilot model which was transported to the *Heereswaffenamt* test ground at Kummersdorf for official army trials. By this time, the Tiger tank had just started in production, but its shortcomings – including

Sloped armour, a 75-mm high velocity gun, wider tracks and improved suspension gave the Panther a chance against the Russian T-34

excessive weight, low speed, and poor ballistic shape – were already recognised. The new vehicle was ordered into immediate production as the PzKpfw V Panther, with the ordnance designation SdKfz 171, and it got absolute top priority rating.

The first vehicle was turned out by MAN in November 1942, only two months after completion of the prototype. It was planned to build at a rate of 250 vehicles a month as soon as possible, but at the end of 1942 this target was increased to 600 a month. To reach such an ambitious target it was necessary to form a large Panther production group. Daimler-Benz were quickly switched from work on their now-discarded Panther design (prototypes of which had by then been almost completed) and in November 1942 they too began tooling up to build

Panthers, the first vehicles coming from Daimler early in 1943.

Also in January 1943, Maschinenfabrik Niedersachsen of Hanover and Henschel, began tooling up to build MAN Panthers – production started in February/March – and scores of sub-contractors were soon involved in what became one of the most concentrated German armaments programmes of the war. Even aircraft production was cut back, partly to conserve fuel for use in tanks but partly, also, to free manufacturing facilities for the urgently needed Panther engines and components.

The monthly target of 600 vehicles was never achieved, however. By May 1943 output had reached a total of 324 completed vehicles and the monthly production average over the year was 154. In 1944 a monthly production average of 330 vehicles was achieved. By February 1945, when production tailed off, 4814 Panthers had been built. Panthers were first used in action in the great Kursk Offensive of 5 July 1943, but the haste with which the design had been evolved, and the speed with which it had been put into production, led to many teething troubles. In particular the complicated track and suspension gave trouble, with frequent breakages, while the engine presented cooling problems and this led to frequent engine fires. In the early months of service, indeed, more Panthers were put out of service by mechanical faults than by Soviet anti-tank guns.

Conventional layout

The Panther conformed to the usual layout of German tanks. It had the driving and transmission compartment forward, the fighting compartment and turret in the centre, and the engine compartment at the rear. The driver sat on the left-hand side forward with a vision port in front of him in the glacis plate. This was fitted with a laminated glass screen and had an armoured hinged flap on the outside which was closed under combat conditions. Forward vision was then given by two fixed episcopes in the compartment roof, one facing directly forward while the other faced half left in the '10–30' position. This restricted vision considerably and in the later Ausf G a rotating periscope was fitted in place of the fixed forward episcope, and the half left episcope and the vision port were completely dispensed with.

The Ausf G was thus easily recognised from the front since it had an unpierced glacis plate. The wireless operator, who was also the hull machine-gunner, sat on the right side forward. In the early Ausf D models, he was provided with a vertical opening flap in the glacis plate – rather similar to a vertical letterbox flap – through which he fired a standard MG 34 machine-gun in action. In the Ausf A and G, however, this arrangement was replaced by an integral ball-mount which took the MG 34 in the standard type of tank mounting. The radio equipment was fitted to the radio-operator/gunner's right and was located in the sponson which overhung the tracks. Episcopes were fitted, duplicating the driver's side.

Between the driver and wireless operator was the gearbox, with final drive which led each side to the front sprockets. The gearbox was specially evolved for the Panther as this vehicle was bulkier and heavier than previous designs and developed considerably more power. Known as the AK 7-200,

the gearbox was an all synchromesh unit with seven speeds. Argus hydraulic disc brakes were used for steering in the conventional manner by braking the tracks. However, the epicyclic gears could also be used to assist steering by driving one or other of the sprockets against the main drive, so retarding the track on that side and allowing sharper radius turns.

In the turret the gunner sat on the left hand side of the gun and was originally provided with an articulated binocular sight; this was later changed to a monocular sight. He fired the gun electrically by a trigger fitted on the elevating handwheel. The coaxial machine-gun, fitted in the mantlet, was fired by the gunner from a foot switch. Traverse was by hydraulic power or hand, the same handwheel being used for either method.

The vehicle commander's station was at

the left rear of the turret, the offset location being necessitated by the length of the breech which virtually divided the turret into two. A prominent cupola was provided which was of the 'dustbin' type with six vision slits in the Ausf D. In the Panther Ausf A and G, however, an improved cupola was fitted which had seven equally-spaced periscopes. This had a hatch which lifted and opened horizontally. Above the cupola was fitted a ring mount for an MG 34 which could be used for air defence, though this mount was sometimes removed.

The remaining crew member was the loader who occupied the right side of the turret. The turret itself had sloped walls and a rounded front covered by a curved cast mantlet. The cage had a full floor which rotated with the turret. Drive for the hydraulic traverse was taken through the centre of the floor to a gearbox, and thence

Armaments Minister Albert Speer tests a Kettenrad tracked motorcycle. His programme of rationalisation was vital to the quantity production of Panthers and Tigers

Panther Armour Disposition

to an oil motor. Turret openings were kept to a minimum and included a large circular hatch on the rear face which was an access/escape hatch for the loader and was also used for loading ammunition. On the left side beneath the cupola was a circular hatch for ejecting expended cartridge cases, but this was eliminated in the Ausf A and G. Similarly eliminated were three small pistol ports, one in each face, which were normally plugged by a steel bung and chain.

The engine, housed in the rear compartment, was a Maybach HL 230 P30, a V-12 23 litre unit of 700 hp at 3000 rpm. This was a bored out version of the HL 210 engine originally planned. The earliest production vehicles had the HL 210 unit, but like most AFV designs, the Panther had increased in weight considerably during the development stage with a heavier gun and heavier armour (among other things) bringing its

weight up from the 35 tons originally envisaged to about 43 (metric) tons. The easy way to increase the power to compensate for the added weight was to enlarge the engine. Access to the engine for maintenance was via a large inspection hatch in the centre of the rear decking. Cooling grilles and fans occupied most of the remainder of the rear decking. Exhaust was taken away through manifolds on the squared off hull rear. Most Panthers had stowage boxes flanking the rear exhaust pipes, but these were not always fitted.

The actual hull and superstructure was a single built-up unit of machinable quality homogenous armour plate of welded construction but with all main edges strengthened by mortised interlocking as had been pioneered in the Tiger. The heaviest armour (80 mm) was on the glacis plate which was sloped at 33° to the horizontal, an angle

specifically selected to deflect shells striking the glacis upwards clear of the mantlet.

The suspension consisted of eight double interleaved bogie wheels on each side, the wheels being dished discs with solid rubber tyres. Some very late production vehicles, however, had all-steel resiliently sprung wheels of the type subsequently fitted to the late production Tiger and the Tiger II (Royal Tiger). The first, third, fifth and seventh wheels from the front were double while the intervening axles carried spaced wheels overlapping the others on the inside and outside. Each bogie axle was joined by a radius arm to a torsion bar coupled in series to a second bar lying parallel to it.

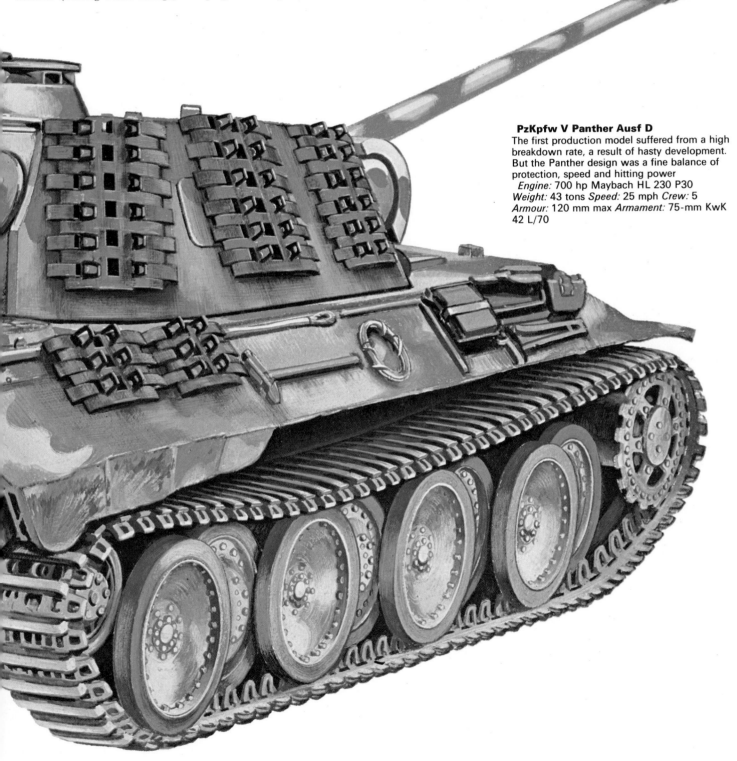

PzKpfw V Panther Ausf D
The first production model suffered from a high breakdown rate, a result of hasty development. But the Panther design was a fine balance of protection, speed and hitting power
Engine: 700 hp Maybach HL 230 P30
Weight: 43 tons *Speed:* 25 mph *Crew:* 5
Armour: 120 mm max *Armament:* 75-mm KwK 42 L/70

The torsion bars were carried across the floor and the bogie wheels on the right hand side of the vehicle were set behind their respective torsion bars while those on the left were set in front. Thus, as in the Tiger, the wheel layout was not symmetrical. Though this suspension was technically advanced and gave the vehicle superb flotation, maintenance was complicated by the size of the wheels and consequent inaccessibility of the axles and torsion bars. Moreover, wheel replacement was a heavy and lengthy task.

The 75-mm L/70 gun mounted in the Panther was developed by Rheinmetall who had been asked in July 1941 to design a high velocity version of the 75-mm weapon which could penetrate 140 mm of armour plate at 1000 metres. This high velocity gun requirement, initially envisaged for a field carriage, was among the weapons considered by the Panzer Commission in their deliberations of November 1941 which gave rise to the VK 3002 (Panther) specification. As a result, Rheinmetall were asked to design the turret and mount to hold this gun for installation in the VK 3002 design. The prototype gun was ready in early 1942, a weapon 60 calibres long. Test firing

indicated that performance was a little below the requested minimum, so the barrel was lengthened to 70 calibres, the improved prototype being ready for tests in June 1942. In this lengthened form the gun went into production. Initially it had a single baffle muzzle brake – and was so used on the earliest Panthers – but later a double baffle muzzle brake was adopted.

Panther production

The first Panther models which came off the MAN line from November 1942 were designated in standard German fashion as PzKpfw V Ausf A. The designation PzKpfw V Ausf B was earmarked for a proposed version of the vehicle which was to have the Maybach-Olvar gearbox in place of the specially developed AK 7-200 unit. However, the Maybach gearbox was considered unsuitable for installation in the Panther and the Ausf B never materialised. The first 20 Panthers which originally had the Ausf A designation were 'pre-production' vehicles. They had the 60 mm thick front armour as originally called for, the Maybach HL 210 engine, also as originally specified, a ZF 7 gearbox with clutch and brake steering, the earliest form of the

L/70 gun, and a cupola bulge in the side of the turret. From January 1943, however, Panthers appeared with all the design improvements suggested from trials with the pilot model. The glacis plate thickness was increased to 80 mm, the bored out HL 230 engine was fitted together with the new AK 7-200 gearbox which allowed single radius turns (ie, a definite fixed radius of turn depending on the gear engaged) and also made a neutral turn possible with the vehicle stationary. To simplify turret production, the cupola was shifted slightly to the right, thus eliminating the bulged housing.

Confused classification

This first full production type was designated PzKpfw V Ausf D. No record has been unearthed of an Ausf C model, but it seems almost certain that this was a 'paper project', like the Ausf B with some other proposed mechanical change. Much confusion has always existed over the designations of these early Panthers mainly because the Germans themselves later classed the early Ausf A vehicles with the full production Ausf Ds for record purposes. Early in 1943 they confused the record

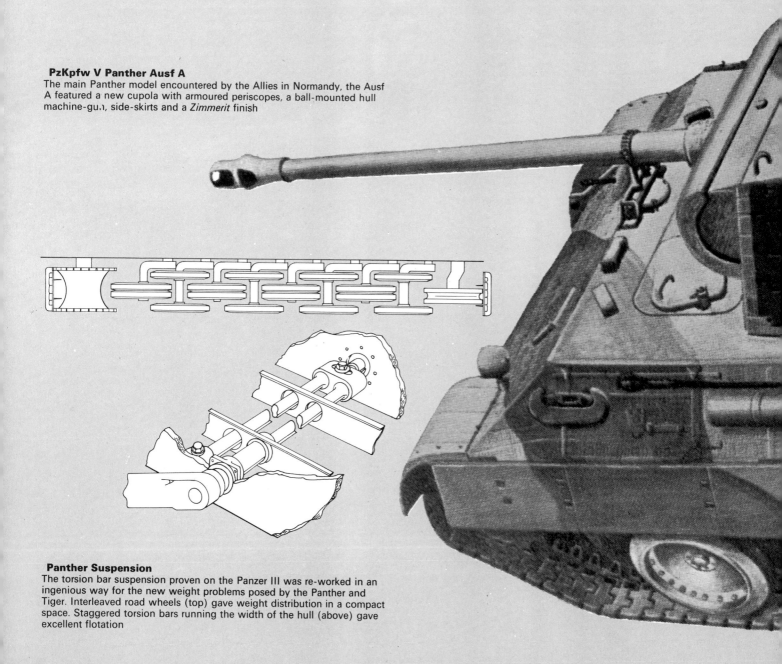

PzKpfw V Panther Ausf A
The main Panther model encountered by the Allies in Normandy, the Ausf A featured a new cupola with armoured periscopes, a ball-mounted hull machine-gun, side-skirts and a *Zimmerit* finish

Panther Suspension
The torsion bar suspension proven on the Panzer III was re-worked in an ingenious way for the new weight problems posed by the Panther and Tiger. Interleaved road wheels (top) gave weight distribution in a compact space. Staggered torsion bars running the width of the hull (above) gave excellent flotation

further by identifying the original Ausf A as the Ausf D1 and the Ausf D as the Ausf D2.

Characteristics of the Ausf D were the 'dustbin' cupola, the vision port and machine-gun port on the glacis, smoke dischargers on the turret sides, and a straight edge to the lower sponson sides with separate stowage compartments fabricated beneath the rear ends. On later Ausf Ds the improved type of cupola was fitted and the smoke dischargers were dropped in favour of a bomb thrower installed in the turret roof and operated by the loader. Later Ausf Ds also had the skirt armour, which was adopted as standard to protect the top run of the tracks from bazooka hits. Zimmerit anti-magnetic paste covering to prevent the attachment of mines was another retrospective feature. All except the earliest vehicles had the L/70 gun with double baffle.

Next production model of the Panther was designated Ausf A, an anomaly which has not been fully explained, but may conceivably have resulted from an early administrative, phonetic, or clerical error, since the logical designation was Ausf E. Be that as it may, the Ausf A appeared in the latter half of 1943 and featured several detail improvements. Chief among these was the adoption of the new cupola with armoured periscopes, and the provision of a proper ball-mount for the hull machine-gun. Side skirts of 5-mm armour and a Zimmerit finish were standard. The side skirts were only loosely fixed by bolts and they were frequently removed, either by the crew or accidentally in combat conditions. The gunner's binocular sight was replaced by a monocular one, though this was not noticeable externally. To further simplify turret production, however, the pistol ports and the small loading hatch featured in the Ausf D were eliminated completely, leaving just the big loading/escape hatch in the turret rear. The Panther Ausf A was the main type encountered by the Allies in the Normandy fighting.

Action in Normandy

The final production model of the Panther in its original form, the Ausf G, was also in action in Normandy in June 1944. By this time the designation PzKpfw V had been dropped following a personal directive from Hitler on 27 February 1944, and the vehicle was simply known as the Panther Ausf G. (At this same time, the Tiger was similarly re-designated as Tiger Ausf E.) Considerable modifications were featured in G models. The superstructure sides were altered, mainly to simplify production, so that the rear stowage compartments were now integral with the hull instead of separate additions. This gave a sloping lower edge to the sponsons. The hull sides were at the same time increased in thickness from 40 mm to 50 mm with the angle of slope altered from 30° to 40°. The driver's vision port was eliminated from the glacis plate and his vision was greatly improved by provision of a rotating periscope in place of the episcopes. New hinged hatches with spring-assisted opening replaced the original hatches provided in the hull roof for the driver and wireless operator. The earlier models had pivoted hatches which were found to jam easily. Internally, armoured ammunition bins were fitted inside each sponson with sliding armoured doors to reduce fire risk. The 75-mm ammunition stowage was also slightly increased in this model from 79 to 82 rounds.

Some amendments were made to external stowage, including the provision of a stronger method of attaching the skirt armour.

In very late production vehicles the cylindrical stowage box for the gun pull-through and cleaning gear was removed from the left side of the hull and mounted across the hull at the rear of the engine compartment. With Tiger and Panther production under way, a new generation of tanks was planned in 1943 which was to incorporate the lessons from existing designs. In particular, attention was to be given to simplifying production, economising on materials, reducing maintenance, and standardising components as far as possible. By this time economic conditions were extremely grim in Germany, with shortages of fuel, raw materials and manpower, and disruption of all aspects of life by continual Allied bombing – not to mention the demands of supplying several hard-pressed fighting fronts at the same time.

In February 1943 Waffenprufamt 6 asked MAN and Henschel to produce improved designs for the Panther and Tiger respectively, ensuring maximum interchangeability of parts. Henschel produced the Tiger II which went into production at the end of 1943 since a replacement for the somewhat unsatisfactory Tiger was urgently needed. The improved Panther, the Panther II, officially designated Panther Ausf F, was to have a hull similar to the existing Panther but with the same form of interleaved all-steel resilient wheels as the Tiger II. Other changes were to be the adoption of an improved gearbox and transmission, the AK 7-400, and mechanical parts such as brakes identical to those in the Tiger II.

Smaller turret
The armour on the hull top was to be doubled to 25 mm and the ball-mount was to be altered to take the MG 42. The major change, however, was to be a new design of turret, known as the *Panzerturm Schmal* (small), which as its name implies was much smaller than the original Panther turret. The object was to reduce weight, simplify production, reduce frontal area, eliminate shot traps beneath the mantlet (a weakness in the original Panther turret) and enable a larger gun to be fitted. It was to have a built-in stereoscopic rangefinder, and a gyrostabiliser for both the sight and the gun based on that fitted in American tanks. As part of the experimental work for this a standard Panther was fitted with a captured American gyrostabiliser for firing trials and proved to have its accuracy and effectiveness doubled.

A major tactical requirement was that any Panther II should be capable of instant conversion in the field to the command tank role by providing the necessary brackets and a second aerial in every turret. This meant that the commander's ultra short wave radio set could be 'plugged in' to any vehicle so that command and staff officers could quickly change to other tanks if theirs were damaged or immobilised.

The new small turret was developed as a separate project by Daimler-Benz under the direction of Dr Wunderlich, assisted by Col Henrici, a gunnery expert from *Waffenprufamt 6*. Kniepkampf was in over-all charge of both the Tiger II and Panther II projects. The new turret proved a most successful design. It had the same ring diameter as the old turret, but took 30% less time to make and had 30% more armour plate all within the same weight limit. It

could take the L/70 gun and was also designed to accommodate a proposed lengthened L/100 version of the same weapon. It could take the same 88-mm gun as the Tiger II as yet another alternative. The wide mantlet, difficult to manufacture, which characterised the old turret, was replaced by a relatively simple *Saukopf* (pig's head) mantlet, of conical shape as its description implies. To fit this conical shape the design of the L/70 gun was modified so that the recuperator and buffer cylinders were situated under the gun. The compressor for the barrel blow-out apparatus was eliminated, and compressed air was obtained instead from an additional cylinder round the recuperator which was kept charged by pressure from the gun recoil.

The result of these changes was that the wide welded cradle in the original Panther turret could be dispensed with completely. It also proved possible to eliminate the muzzle brake with the new small turret, even though the recoil forces were massively increased from 12 to 18 tons.

The *schmal* turret was ready before the Panther II, but though running prototypes of this vehicle were produced in 1944, the rapidly deteriorating conditions of the war with facilities curtailed and the need for continued supply of types already proven in service meant that the Panther II, or Ausf F, never went into production and there was thus no chance for this fine design, virtually a perfected version of the original Panther, to prove its mettle. It would have undoubtedly been a much more useful and potent weapon than the very heavy and bulky Tiger II.

Final production models of the Panther Ausf G did, in fact, incorporate one feature intended for the Ausf F. This was the all-steel resilient road wheel which replaced the rubber-tyred type and became standard for late-production Tigers as well as the Tiger II. It is apposite also to mention here the engine improvements which were gradually introduced for the Maybach HL 230 motor. Overheating had been a problem in the early days, as previously mentioned. This was overcome by fitting a second cooling pump, modifying the coolant distribution, and improving the bearings and cylinder head seal. Later Panthers, therefore, proved very much more reliable than the vehicles involved in the Kursk debacle. To improve the power of the HL 230 for the Tiger II and Panther II it was proposed to increase the compression ratio and incorporate fuel injection and, later, superchargers. Though modified prototypes were built and tested, the war had ended before the up-rated engine could go into production.

Special conversions
There were several special purpose conversions of the Panther, two of these for the command role. For unit commanders the *Befehlspanzer* Panther was produced. These were simply versions of either the Ausf D, A or G fitted with extra radio equipment and the associated aerials. A second radio receiver and transmitter were fitted to the inside right wall of the turret and the loader acted as operator. There were two externally similar models, differing only in the radio installation. The SdKfz 267 had Fu 5 and Fu 8 equipment, while the SdKfz 268 had Fu 5 and Fu 7. (Fu 5 was the standard German tank wire-

Below: Schmalturm on a test rig. Note the tube-frame turret cage. The projected turret for the second generation Panther, in spite of being lighter and smaller, was designed to take a larger gun. The saukopf mantlet and sloped armour gave very good defensive qualities. Top right: A Panther is given an engine change by a half-track mobile gantry. Below right: Panther Ausf G, with side track skirts and a generous cover of Zimmerit anti-magnetic mine paste coating

Peter Chamberlain

less for short-range communication within tank regiments and battalions on RT or MCW transmission. Fu 7 was the standard air co-operation set and Fu 8 was the set used for main divisional nets. [Fu = *Funk* = Radio].) In each case ammunition stowage was reduced to 64 75-mm rounds. *Befehlspanzer* Panthers were used by regimental and battalion command and staff officers and could only be distinguished externally by the extra aerials (or the call sign number when this was visible).

The *Beobachtungspanzer* Panther (SdKfz 172) was an old Ausf D converted as an OP vehicle for observation officers, commanders, and staff officers of SP artillery regiments. The gun was replaced by a short wooden dummy, the turret was fixed in place, an extra radio was fitted, and a map table was added inside the turret. A ball-mounted MG 34 in the turret front was the only armament.

Finally there was the *Bergepanzer* Panther (also known as the *Bergepanther*), designated SdKfz 179, which was a recovery vehicle specially for work with tanks in the 45-ton class. The *Bergepanther* replaced the 18-ton half-track in the heavy recovery role, since it took up to three of these latter vehicles to move heavy tanks like the Tiger or Panther. The *Bergepanther* was an old Ausf D model converted by the removal of the turret and the fighting equipment. A movable winch and winch motor were installed in the fighting compartment. A limited superstructure was provided round the former turret opening consisting of heavy wood cladding over mild steel framing. A canvas tilt could cover the complete compartment in bad weather. An 'A' frame was fitted over the rear decking and this supported a towing eye and towing rollers. A heavy earth spade was hinged on the hull rear and was raised and lowered from the vehicle's winch. There was a light demountable jib which could be erected either side for lifting work and there was an MG 34

Tritschler (Opera Mundi)

Bundesarchiv

or a 20-mm cannon for air defence, mounted as required.

Had the war dragged on (and had Germany been able to maintain its planned production programme unhindered), the Panther and Panther II would have become the backbone of the German panzer divisions (together with the Tiger II and *Jagdtiger* in lesser numbers), and from late 1944 a rationalisation programme was introduced (*Richtwert-Programm* IV) which terminated production of all earlier types in favour of the 'new generation' vehicles. The other type to be included in the new programme was a family of *Waffentragers* and SP types developed on a light chassis adapted from the Czech-built PzKpfw 38(t) (and its German-developed derivative the 38(d)).

However, the defeat of Germany in May 1945 brought Panther development to an end with much of the potential of the design still unrealised. A few Panthers served on

for a number of post-war years in the French Army, which equipped some units with captured vehicles. The other victorious nations each took a few Panthers for trials. The British actually built at least one Panther in 1946, using spare and cannibalised parts to assemble a 'new' vehicle which was used in comparative trials with the Black Prince and Centurion.

An interesting clandestine use of the Panther took place during the last desperate German offensive in the West, the so-called 'Battle of the Bulge'. Here at least ten, probably more, Panthers were effectively disguised and marked to resemble US Army M10 tank destroyers. The cupola was removed, together with the external stowage boxes on the hull. The turret and nose were then disguised with thin sheet metal to resemble the shape of the M10, including the distinctive rear overhang of that vehicle's turret counterweight. Despite being finished in very convincing US markings,

the phoney M10s enjoyed little success largely because the subtlety of the idea was nullified by the general confusion prevailing – on both sides – during the frantic days of the Ardennes offensive.

Japan purchased a Panther with a view to producing licence-built versions for use in the Pacific. Colonel Ishide, an AFV specialist with the Japanese Military Mission to Germany, witnessed a demonstration of both a Tiger I and a Panther at the Henschel works on 30 July 1943. As a result the Japanese bought one sample of each vehicle with the intention of shipping them to Japan for further trials and probable production of their own versions. This transaction took place in November 1944 when a Tiger and Panther were formally handed over to the Japanese Mission in Germany. However, by this time there was no means of getting these vehicles safely to Japan and as far as is known they never actually left Germany.

TIGER II
THE KING PANZER

The original Tiger design was finalised before the Soviet T-34 was encountered so it lacked the excellent ballistic shape which was a feature of the Panther. In late 1942 when the first Tigers had entered service, *Waffenamt* asked Henschel if they could produce a modified design with sloping side plates as in the new Panther. By February 1943 the mechanical failings of the Tiger had been revealed and a development specification for a replacement vehicle was issued under the designation VK 4502.

Porsche offered a design, the VK 4502 (P), which had alternative layouts with the turret either well forward or at the back of the hull. These were designated Types 180 and 181 by Porsche. The new vehicle was to mount the longer L/71 KwK 43 gun as in the *Elefant* tank destroyer. A turret design was put in hand by Wegmann of Kassel. Porsche once again offered petrol-electric drive for the Type 180, and once again this was rejected by *Waffenamt* as unreliable and too sophisticated for service conditions. In addition a shortage of copper ruled out electric transmission.

Henschel also put forward a design, the VK 4503 (H), to meet the requirement, and this was powered conventionally like their Tiger. This design was accepted and the project was put in hand as a top priority

effort. The design was not finalised until October 1943, however, three months later than scheduled. This happened because the Panther II had since been designed, and under the new rationalisation policy it was decided that as many parts of the Panther II as possible had to be incorporated, and design features were to be standardised between the two vehicles.

Turret changes
The prototype of the new tank, now designated PzKpfw Tiger Ausf B, was ready in November 1943 and the first production models appeared in February 1944 on the Henschel production line, parallel to that which was still building the Tiger Ausf E. Ironically enough, history repeated itself when the first 50 of the new vehicles mounted the Porsche turret, now surplus from the cancelled Type 180. All subsequent Tiger Ausf Bs had a Henschel-designed turret, which was of more simple construction than the Porsche model, and it avoided the Porsche turret's built-in shot-trap under the mantlet.

Henschel remained the sole builders of the Tiger Ausf B during its whole production life. By September 1944 Tiger Ausf E production ceased completely in favour of the new vehicle. At this particular time a

production rate of 100, increasing to 145, vehicles a month had been fixed. In practice, however, disruption by enemy bombing and shortage of materials meant the best ever monthly output, in August 1944, was only 84. By March 1945, this total had fallen to 25. Final total of Tiger Ausf Bs produced was 484.

Although the official designation was PzKpfw Tiger Ausf B (SdKfz 182) it was variously known as the *Königstiger* (King Tiger), or Tiger II to the Germans, and as the Royal Tiger to the Allies. The King Tiger went into action for the first time in Normandy in June 1944, and the first was knocked out by the Allies in the August of that year.

The King Tiger was derived from the Tiger Ausf E and both tanks had many features in common. At the same time it bore a much closer resemblance to the late model Panther and the projected Panther Ausf F (Panther II), which was due for production in 1945. Many fittings were standard to both the King Tiger and the late model Panther and Tiger. These included cupolas, engines, engine covers and road wheels, to mention just a few. Compared with the other vehicles, the King Tiger had thicker armour (maximum 150 mm) and was dimensionally larger. There

was a small, conical *Saukopf* (pig's head) mantlet, and a well-sloped turret and sloped morticed armour plates making up the hull. Main armament was the 88-mm KwK 43 (L/61) as fitted to the *Elefant*.

Internally the vehicle followed the usual German layout with front sprocket drive and crew positions as for the Panther. The big turret had several interesting features – it lacked the usual basket and was built out very wide over an immense 73-in diameter

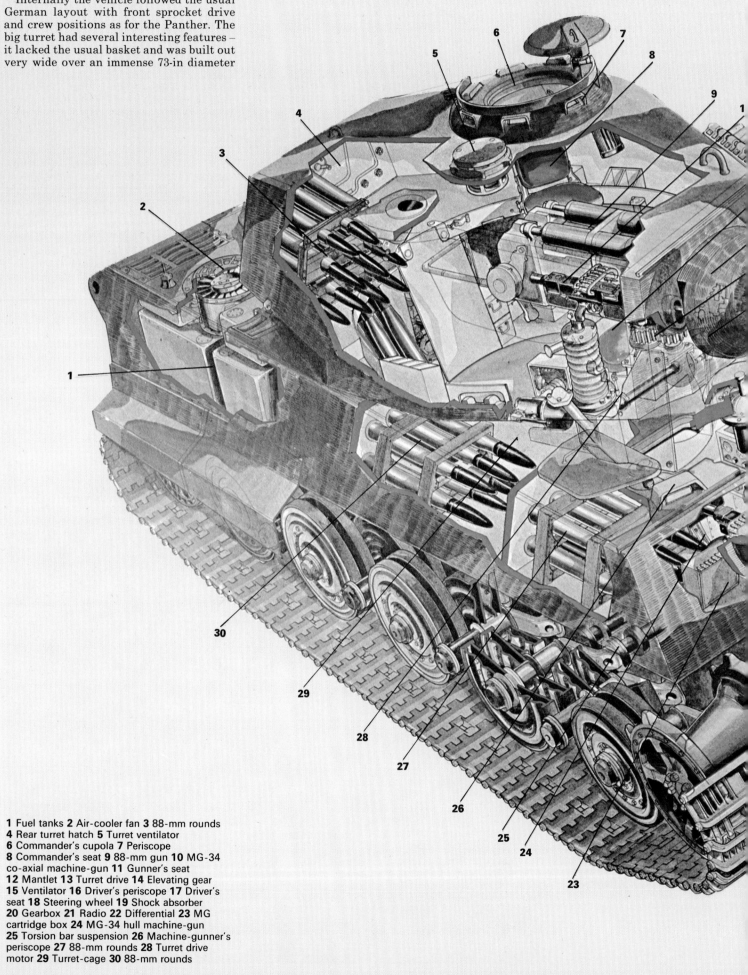

1 Fuel tanks **2** Air-cooler fan **3** 88-mm rounds
4 Rear turret hatch **5** Turret ventilator
6 Commander's cupola **7** Periscope
8 Commander's seat **9** 88-mm gun **10** MG-34 co-axial machine-gun **11** Gunner's seat
12 Mantlet **13** Turret drive **14** Elevating gear
15 Ventilator **16** Driver's periscope **17** Driver's seat **18** Steering wheel **19** Shock absorber
20 Gearbox **21** Radio **22** Differential **23** MG cartridge box **24** MG-34 hull machine-gun
25 Torsion bar suspension **26** Machine-gunner's periscope **27** 88-mm rounds **28** Turret drive motor **29** Turret-cage **30** 88-mm rounds

turret ring. To assist in loading the big ammunition rounds carried, 22 ready-for-use rounds were mounted, 11 per side, in the rear turret bulge, thus giving the loader a minimum handling movement. Power traverse was as for the Panther and Tiger.

Suspension was by torsion bars and it followed the same type of arrangement as in the Tiger Ausf E. But, the wheels were overlapped rather than interleaved as on the Tiger E. This change was adapted to simplify the maintenance problems which

had been inherent with interleaved road wheels. Similarly, the tendency for the wheels to freeze solid with packed snow was obviated to some extent. Steel-tyred resiliently sprung wheels (which featured a layer of rubber between two steel tyres) were standard on the King Tiger as on the late model Tiger Es and Panthers. A commander's version of the King Tiger, differing only in internal radio stowage, was also produced and it carried the designation of *Befehlspanzer* Tiger B.

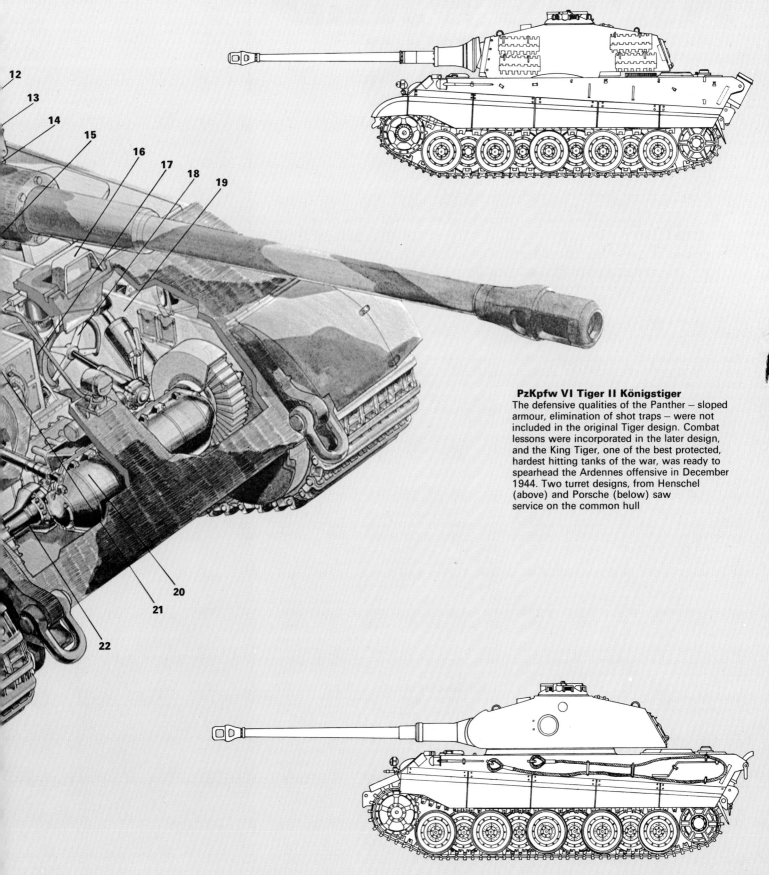

PzKpfw VI Tiger II Königstiger
The defensive qualities of the Panther – sloped armour, elimination of shot traps – were not included in the original Tiger design. Combat lessons were incorporated in the later design, and the King Tiger, one of the best protected, hardest hitting tanks of the war, was ready to spearhead the Ardennes offensive in December 1944. Two turret designs, from Henschel (above) and Porsche (below) saw service on the common hull

SUPER HEAVY TANKS
THE ARMOURED GIANTS

The structure of the German tank industry was anything but super-efficient. Partisans of rival schemes fluttered around Hitler's court to win approval for grandiose new projects. Thus the 'mad inventors' had their day and the super-heavy tanks were born . . .

The obsession with size culminated in a series of super-heavy tanks of gigantic proportion. Porsche was the driving force behind the first of these, the *Maus*, while the second type to be built, the E 100, was sponsored by the *Heereswaffenamt* as a competitive design.

First consideration of a super-heavy tank was made in late 1941, when Dr Ferdinand Porsche was at his most influential with Hitler. Porsche drew up a project which he called *Maus* (Mouse) and in August 1943, he got approval, again directly from Hitler, to go ahead and build a prototype. At this time Porsche's personal stock was low with the *Waffenamt*; he was removed as head of the Panzer Commission and none of his designs had been selected for production.

Hitler possibly thought that the *Maus* project would recompense Porsche for the past failures, or at least keep him away from other projects. Also, at this period, Hitler was still enthusiastic about the super-heavy tank, and his armaments minister, Albert Speer, had endorsed the idea.

Tank inventor's dream
The *Maus* was a tank inventor's dream, a wild extravagance of design, in short the ultimate example of the divergence of ideas between the designer of little knowledge of tactical requirements and the men with practical experience. The resultant vehicle weighed 180 tons, was over 30 ft long and had 240 mm thickness of frontal armour. A special engine of 1200 hp was designed by Daimler and was tested in both its diesel and petrol forms in two prototypes.

True to Porsche's previous designs, the *Maus* had electric transmission, and the internal layout, with central engine, was similar to that of the *Elefant*, which had been produced from the Tiger (P). The armour was made up of flat rolled plates and the main plates were mortised and welded together. The turret had a rounded front made from a single bent plate, 93 mm thick. The rear plate of the turret was slightly sloped.

Special equipment
Maximum road speed, via electric generators under the turret floor, was 12½ mph. There were 48 partly interleaved wheels in four sets of four wheel bogies providing the suspension, and over-all track height was low in relation to the size of the vehicle. The axles of each set of bogies were sprung, and each bogie was set on a longitudinal torsion bar. The vehicle was gas proof and it could wade to a depth of 26 ft using a snorkel tube to provide air. The snorkel installation was to allow the *Maus* to cross rivers, for few bridges could take the weight of the monster.

The designed turret weighed 50 tons (the weight of a complete Centurion tank) and the armament was a 128-mm gun (as fitted to the *Jagdtiger* tank destroyer) plus a 75-mm gun mounted co-axially. The first turret was not completed, in fact, until the middle of 1944, and the two prototypes completed trials with weighted simulated turrets.

Initially the *Maus* project was known under the code name *Mammut* (Mammoth) and Krupp were contracted to build it. The first prototype was completed in November 1943 and the dummy turret was added the following month. Trials were held

An early prototype of Maus, Dr Ferdinand Porsche's idea of a super heavy tank. Pressures on the German war industry led to work on it being halted in 1944, and the prototypes were blown up in the last weeks of the war in Europe–

Chris Ellis

in the winter, lasting until May 1944. The following month the second prototype was delivered. Trials took place at Krupp's test area in Meppen.

Development abandoned

Two more hulls were under construction during the closing months of the war and a total of six vehicles were known to have been ordered. But, in the last year of war, work on the *Maus* virtually stopped. In April 1944, Hitler personally ordered that all work on giant tank projects was to cease in favour of devoting all resources to building established proven tanks like the Panther and King Tiger. The *Maus* prototypes were blown up in the last weeks of the war as the Russians closed in on Meppen. Guns, turrets, hulls and test firing rigs were found by Allied Intelligence officers abandoned and partially destroyed.

Porsche and the tank's builders, Krupp, had not stopped at producing the *Maus*, however, for design studies were found at Krupp for tanks of 110, 130, 150 and 170 tons and all carried the designation 'Krupp-Maus'. Also discovered was a project study for a version of the *Maus* carrying a 305-mm breech-loading mortar. The project was named 'Bear'. The most fantastic of all, however, was a preliminary layout for a giant 1500-ton vehicle with an 800-mm gun as main armament and two 15-cm guns in auxiliary turrets on the rear quarters. Frontal armour was to be 250 mm at 45° and it was planned to power this monster with four submarine diesel engines.

The E 100 project was virtually the *Heereswaffenamt* rival to the *Maus*. There was considerable opposition to Porsche and his unconventional mechanical ideas within the Ordnance Department, and no

opportunity was lost to play down his projects.

Under Heydekampf at the Panzer Commission a long-term plan to produce a rationalised series of 'new generation' tanks was drawn up, the so-called *Entwicklungtypen* or E series. This range of tanks was to use standardised parts and was to be built in classes of varying sizes to replace existing vehicles. Types were as follows:

Designation	Weight class
E 10	10–15 tons
E 25	25–30 tons
E 50	50 tons (Panther replacement)

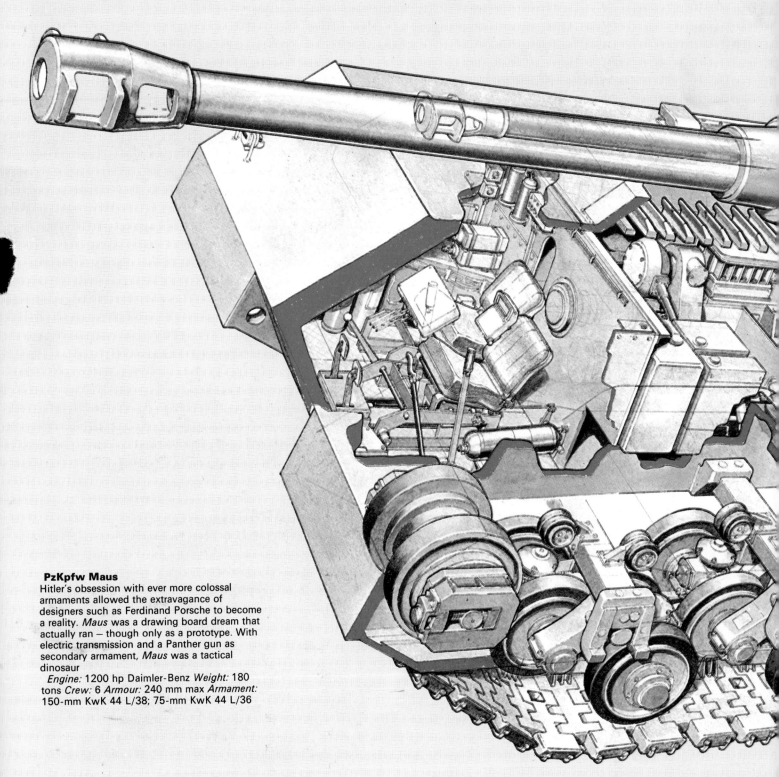

PzKpfw Maus
Hitler's obsession with ever more colossal armaments allowed the extravagance of designers such as Ferdinand Porsche to become a reality. *Maus* was a drawing board dream that actually ran — though only as a prototype. With electric transmission and a Panther gun as secondary armament, *Maus* was a tactical dinosaur
Engine: 1200 hp Daimler-Benz *Weight:* 180 tons *Crew:* 6 *Armour:* 240 mm max *Armament:* 150-mm KwK 44 L/38; 75-mm KwK 44 L/36

E 75	75 tons (Tiger/King Tiger replacement)
E 100	130–140 tons (super heavy type)

Of these only the E 100 project was actually started. This appears to have come about purely as an attempt to rival Porsche's work. When Porsche started work on the *Maus*, the first action of *Heereswaffenamt* was to place an instant contract with Henschel, builders of the King Tiger, for a much enlarged, super-heavy version of the King Tiger. This project was known unofficially as the *Tiger-Maus* and officially as the *Löwe* (Lion) or VK 7001. The armament was to be the same 128-mm gun as the *Jagdtiger*.

With the *Entwicklungtypen* programme drawn up, opportunity was taken to cancel the VK 7001 in favour of the E 100. The E 100 was to be a 140-ton tank with the same turret and gun layout as the *Maus*, except that a 150-mm gun was envisaged as the main weapon. Tiger engines and transmission were specified for the prototype, but an enlarged Maybach engine, the HL 234, was to be developed for production vehicles.

E 100 construction
Road wheels, sprockets and idlers were to be similar to those used on the King Tiger, as was the basic hull shape. Armoured covers were proposed for the tracks, which were one metre wide. To keep the vehicle narrow enough to fit inside the railway loading gauge, the track covers and outer idlers and sprockets were removable. Also, narrow travelling tracks were to be fitted

as on the Tiger. Removable folding jibs on the turret sides were to be used for removing the track covers as required.

After Hitler's order that work on super-heavy projects was to cease, construction of the E 100 prototype proceeded slowly at Henschel's test plant at Haustenbeck, Paderborn. Parts were delayed by the confused industrial situation in Germany during the last year of the war, and at the cessation of hostilities in May 1945 only the bare hull and suspension was partially completed. This was captured by the British, and the E 100 project ceased prematurely. Thus the last of the super-heavy tanks was still-born, and the remainder of the projected 'E' series designs never got beyond the initial drawing board stage. Like National Socialist Germany the development of armoured vehicles had reached the end of the road.

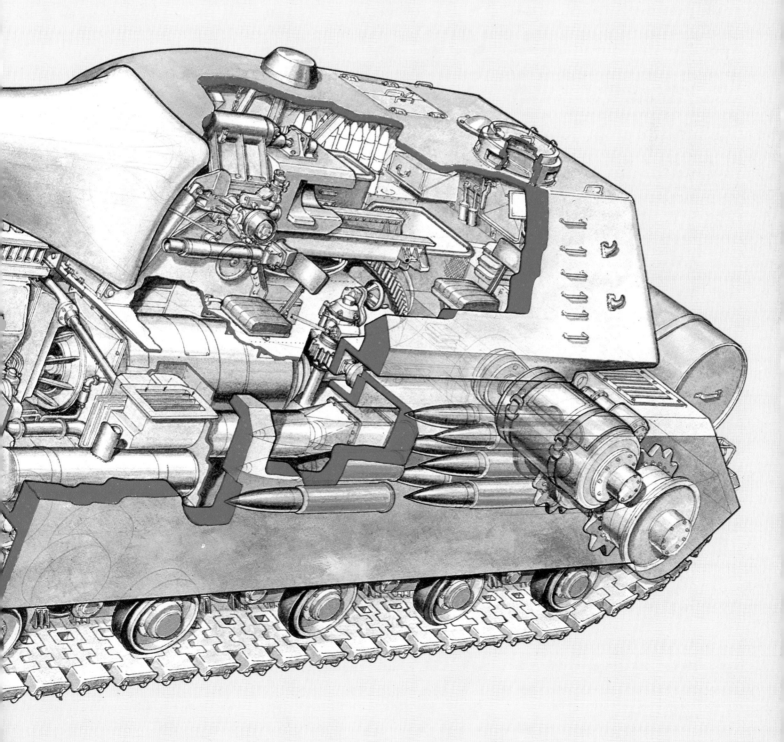

MOBILE SUPPORT

Self-propelled guns on tracked chassis date back almost to the invention of the tank. The very first self-propelled gun was British, the Gun Carrier Mk I of 1916, brainchild of the ingenious men of the Landships Committee who sponsored Britain's first tanks in 1915–16. The Gun Carrier Mk I was the progenitor of all self-propelled guns, and by carrying a complete 60-pounder gun and its carriage in demountable form, it was also the direct ancestor of the *Waffenträger* (weapons carrier) type of vehicle which the Germans also developed during the Second World War.

While some 48 vehicles of this type were built by the British, they rarely used them for their intended role; instead, they were relegated to supply carrying duties. But although the British did not persevere with them, the French Army took up the idea and made all the running in 1916–18. By the time of the Armistice there were about eight self-propelled gun types in French service, usually with a chassis based on the Holt Caterpillar derived type (St Chamond) which had inspired the early French tank efforts. Calibres of the French self-propelled pieces ranged from 280-mm down to 75-mm. The 75-mm version was built on the Renault FT 17 chassis, while larger pieces were on Holt-type chassis. As it happened, two of the largest equipments developed in 1917, the 280-mm and 194-mm guns, remained in French service throughout the inter-war period and were still in use in 1940. The French, however, had made no design progress with self-propelled guns, so there were no successors to these weapons.

American developments
However, the US Army took over where the French left off. When the Americans entered the Great War in 1917, training and supply of the American Expeditionary Force were jointly undertaken by the British and French. The Americans used a number of self-propelled guns (or 'gun motor carriages' as they called them) of the French type, and built others of their own based closely on the French ideas. The resulting pieces were essentially big guns in open mounts on tracked chassis.

Various prototypes were produced until 1922, when development ceased as a result of major cuts in defence expenditure. Around a dozen self-propelled pieces of various calibres were built, from a 240-mm howitzer down to a 75-mm gun. Conclusions drawn by the American Caliber Board – set up to investigate future artillery policy in the 1920s – was that self-propelled guns had a major drawback: the vulnerability of the motorised carriage. If this broke down or was damaged in action then the gun itself was immobilised. The Caliber Board suggested all future artillery should be tractor-hauled and for the rest of the inter-war period only nominal experimental work in self-propelled guns took place. During the Second World War, however, the Americans revived gun motor carriages in a big way.

In Britain in the 1920s there was a short period of revival for self-propelled guns which coincided with the forward-looking period of the Experimental Mechanised Force. Some efficient and compact self-propelled 18-pounders were built on the Vickers chassis of the medium Mk I tank, then in British Army service. The idea for the prototypes was encouraged by the Director of Artillery and, indeed, the main prototype was called the 'Birch Gun' after the then Master-General of the Ordnance. The very first self-propelled guns in the modern sense, the prototypes had an up-to-date purpose-built chassis comparable in performance and standards to contemporary tanks.

The new guns (only three were built) operated experimentally as an integral part of the Mechanised Force on exercises and received world-wide publicity. The Birch Gun looked dramatic, purposeful and efficient. However, although well ahead of any previous thinking, and greatly in advance of the rather crude French and American motor carriages, it was not well received in the British Army. The Royal Artillery were suspicious, and the Tank Corps saw them as usurping tanks on the battlefield (similar differences of opinion held up British self-propelled gun development again during the war), so these promising designs were not pursued. The best self-propelled guns in the British Army in 1939 were a few 'support tanks' which could fire smoke shells by replacing the 2-pounder gun with a 3-in howitzer, and no British self-propelled artillery was even under development in the early stages of the war.

While the German Panzer Divisions were being built up in the 1930s the problem of divisional artillery was not overlooked. But priority was given to calibre and efficiency rather than mobility. To a large extent the problem was one of economics. Tanks or any other type of specialised tracked vehicle were extremely costly and priority was given to tank production. It was much cheaper to use wheeled vehicles to tow artillery pieces than to provide tracked carriages or tractors.

However, prewar German tacticians had not discounted the idea of self-propelled guns, and various prototypes were produced in the 1930s, including an armoured half-track tank destroyer in 1935. None of these was put into production, but the desire for mobile anti-tank guns within Panzer Divisions led to the very swift introduction of a new class of vehicle in 1940, the *Panzerjäger* I (tank hunter) which was based on the Panzer I chassis with an anti-tank gun replacing the original tank turret. This was the first of an increasing number of *Panzerjäger* vehicles which were turned out in rapid succession over the next few years. These were the most important of the early German self-propelled guns. While the *Panzerjäger* were a valued additional weapon in the French campaign in 1940, they became essential after the start of the Russian campaign in 1941. Here thousands of Russian tanks were encountered; the attrition rate on both sides was enormous,

and numbers of fighting vehicles were improvised by fitting guns to obsolescent or captured tank chassis.

The most powerful anti-tank gun available at this time was the Russian 76·2-mm weapon, large numbers of which were captured by the Germans in the early stages of the invasion of the Soviet Union. This was adapted to fit old PzKpfw II and PzKpfw 38(t) chassis. Work started on the new vehicles in December 1941, Alkett converting the PzKpfw IIs and Bohmisch-Mahrische of Prague the PzKpfw 38(t)s. Guns and mounts were adapted by Rheinmetall-Borsig. These vehicles, SdKfz 131 and 132 respectively, were subsequently better known as the *Marder* (marten) II and III.

Plans were made to employ the German 50-mm Pak 38 gun in a similar manner, but this was dropped in favour of the more powerful new 75-mm Pak 40 which was comparable to the Russian gun. In mid-1942 this gun appeared in a more elaborate conversion (also SdKfz 131) on the later model Panzer II chassis. The capture of much French equipment in 1940 led to a similar conversion for the so-called (by the Germans) *Lorraine Schlepper* in 1942, the firm of Becker adding Pak 40 guns and superstructure to make the SdKfz 135, better known as the *Marder* I.

Makeshift conversions
Of necessity these *Panzerjäger* conversions were hasty, crude, and makeshift and from the outset they were regarded as stopgaps while purpose-built vehicles were developed. High silhouettes, thin armour, poor crew protection, low speed, and instability were recognised defects. Improved models based on the PzKpfw 38(t) chassis were the SdKfz 138 and 139, the *Marder* III. They had better armour disposition but still used the tank chassis virtually unchanged. Meanwhile work was undertaken on the basic PzKpfw 38(t) chassis to make it more suitable for the SP role; the rear engine was moved to the middle allowing a larger fighting compartment to be built at the rear and a lower silhouette. Vehicles using this chassis, also designated *Marder* III, appeared in 1943. This was the last of the important *Marder* family, for in 1944 it was succeeded by the *Hetzer*, a fully armoured low silhouette vehicle purpose-built for the anti-tank role.

The new type of anti-tank vehicle introduced the final classification, the *Jagdpanzer* (hunting tank), a type intended to supersede the *Panzerjäger*, even though this aim was never realised. Tank destroyer versions of the Panther and Tiger fell into this category. At this stage the classification of anti-tank vehicles by type became more complicated and terminology was changed by the Germans. Some types originally designated *Panzerjäger* (eg the *Elefant*) were already fully armoured and were re-designated *Jagdpanzer*, into which category the fully armoured assault guns (*Sturmgeschütze*) were also subsequently placed.

Then, at the beginning of 1945, there was

SdKfz 139 'Marder' III
The first *Panzerjäger* 38(t) mounted the Russian
76·2-mm Pak 36(r) on the PzKpfw 38(t) chassis

a further change. All the fully armoured vehicles with a tank destroyer capability were now redesignated as *Panzerjäger* while the erstwhile (and by now obsolescent) *Panzerjäger* of the *Marder* type were recategorised as Pak (Sf) or 'anti-tank carriages'. There were also a number of less well-armed vehicles, mainly based on captured infantry carriers, which had lighter guns. These were mainly used for police work, home defence, or patrol work in occupied countries. A small number of *Panzerjäger* with heavier calibre guns were produced (notably the *Nashorn* [Rhinoceros] and *Elefant*) as well as a new generation of *Panzerjägerkanone* under development in 1945, based on improved versions of the PzKpfw 38 chassis.

The basic unit for *Panzerjäger* deployment was the company, which was subdivided into platoons. Due to their vulnerability it was usual to protect the flanks or rear of a *Panzerjäger* company with infantry, tanks, or towed anti-tank guns. On

the offensive, *Panzerjäger* were used to follow up an attack rather than lead, and they protected against breakthroughs by enemy tanks or picked off retreating stragglers. Platoons or companies usually fired en masse for maximum effect as directed by radio by the company commander, individual platoons engaging different targets as necessary.

On the defensive *Panzerjäger* were kept concealed (but not dug in) as much as possible and were held as mobile reserve to guard against breakthroughs by enemy tanks. File, line, or arrowhead deployment was used. In the last year of the war attacks from the air became a major limitation on the deployment of *Panzerjäger* in the field, these open vehicles being particularly vulnerable to strafing. Infantry, motorised infantry, and later *Volksgrenadier* divisions all had *Panzerjäger* companies, and they were also found in armoured divisions before being displaced by *Jagdpanzer*. Heavier

vehicles like the *Nashorn* and *Elefant* were found in GHQ companies. Despite their tactical limitations, *Panzerjäger* provided fire power and movement in the anti-tank role and played a major part in German armoured warfare operations throughout the Second World War.

While the *Panzerjäger* class of vehicle was the most important, and most numerous, there was parallel development in mobile support artillery, furnished principally for Panzer and Motorised Divisions but later found in nearly all types of fighting division. With tanks and tank hunters in service, the towed artillery now lacked comparable mobility and just as the *Panzerjäger* was quickly improvised by mounting an anti-tank gun on an old tank chassis, so assault howitzers (*Sturmhaubitze*) and infantry guns (*Infanterie Geschütze*) vehicles were produced by placing existing types of howitzer or gun on modified tank chassis.

The first to see service was the 150-mm

L/12 mounted on a Panzer I chassis. This was converted and in service with the Panzer Divisions by the time of the invasion of France in 1940, and enabled the infantry gun companies of Panzer Divisions (six guns to a company) to exchange their tractor-drawn 150-mm infantry guns for the same weapon on a highly mobile chassis. It was a very top heavy and unsatisfactory conversion but it proved the point and led to better things. By 1942 production of self-propelled infantry guns or howitzers was in full swing, the most famous and widely used being the *Wespe* (Wasp) on the PzKpfw II chassis, and the *Hummel* (Bumble Bee) on the PzKpfw III/IV chassis. These self-propelled infantry guns took second place to the tank hunters in priority of output and allocation, but nonetheless usually at least one artillery battalion in a Panzer Division was fully equipped with self-propelled guns.

A later, but similar, type was the self-propelled field howitzer or gun (*Feld-haubitze* or *Feldkanone*), which featured a lighter field piece, also on an obsolete tank chassis. Collectively these SP infantry support weapons were called *Panzer-artillerie* (armoured artillery) and the type of vehicle so produced was known as a *Geschützwagen* (motor-gun), GW for short.

The other major category of self-propelled gun was the *Sturmgeschütze* (assault gun), the one type of tracked artillery vehicle to be purpose-built. Development of assault guns started before the outbreak of war as an integral part of the Panzer Division idea, and a type expressly intended to supplement the towed infantry gun. True mobile support vehicles, with a gun in a tank type mount in a low-profile superstructure, they had a common chassis with the battle tanks – the *Sturmgeschütz* III, (StuG III) was mounted on the PzKpfw III chassis, and the *Sturmgeschütz* IV (StuG IV) on the PzKpfw IV chassis. Indeed, had the German arms industry been geared up for a long war in 1939–40, there would not have been such a vast output of crude improvised types.

It was originally intended that the *Sturmgeschütz* type should supply all the needs of mobile support artillery. They were therefore organised in batteries for allocation by local group commanders to support infantry battalions in the attack. The first two *Sturmgeschütz* battalions were in service for the invasion of France in 1940, and thereafter they became of increasing importance. Assault guns gave the infantry fast-moving firepower, leaving tanks to engage other tanks or spearhead fast-moving thrusts into the enemy flanks.

The assault gun, with a low velocity 75-mm gun, inevitably grew in power: later the high velocity long 75-mm gun was fitted, giving them an effective anti-tank capacity as well, so that there was a merging of the functions of the *Sturmgeschütz* and the *Panzerjäger*. By the latter part of the war there was much intermixing of types and functions, and the *Sturmgeschütz* found itself increasingly replacing tanks.

In fact, the Wehrmacht found the merging of capabilities very useful, for the *Sturmge-schütze* could carry a heavier gun in its

Wespe in action. This self-propelled infantry gun mounted a 105-mm gun on a PzKpfw II chassis

JgPz Tiger (P) 'Elefant'
The most famous of Germany's 'Hunting tanks',
Dr Porsche's 'Elefant' was a formidable weapon
Length: 26·71 ft *Width:* 11·25 ft *Weight:*
158,000 lb *Speed:* 12·5 mph *Range:* 95 miles
Armour: 200 mm max *Armament:* 88-mm Pak 43/2

limited traverse mount than a tank of corresponding size, it was of lower silhouette, had better armour, and was less expensive and quicker to build – all important factors as time and money began to run out. In the latter part of the war *Sturmgeschütze* sometimes partially replaced tanks in tank battalions, and were used to counter enemy tanks. The *Sturmgeschütz* was, of course, greatly superior to the improvised types, and the lessons were quickly learned by the Soviets, who directly copied the German ideas to produce their famous series of SUs (*Samochodnaya Ustanovka* or self-propelled gun) such as the SU-85 and SU-100 (on the T-34 tank chassis) and the SU-122 and SU-152 (on the KV and Josef Stalin tank chassis).

These Russian assault guns, mounting even heavier weapons than the German *Sturmgeschütz*, proved formidable weapons, able to combine all the functions of several types of SP gun in just a few basic types. Even the British Army toyed with the assault gun idea, and a very effectively-armed, though slow, tank destroyer/assault gun version of the Churchill tank was built (the Churchill 3-in gun carrier); this, however, never saw service, mainly due to argument as to whether it should be a Royal Artillery or Tank Corps responsibility.

Closely allied to the *Sturmgeschütze* were one or two less important classes of vehicle which in most cases were built in quite small numbers. These included the *Sturmpanzer* (assault tank) and *Sturmmörser* (assault mortar), both evolved for street fighting on the Eastern Front where the Russians stubbornly held towns and cities street by street – the experience at Stalingrad in 1942 leading directly to their development.

Lastly, and most importantly, came the anti-aircraft tank or *Flakpanzer*, which was developed in the latter part of the war. As we have seen, there were several types of AA mounting on half-tracks, armoured, semi-armoured or unarmoured. As Allied air strength increased from 1943 onwards, these half-track AA vehicles were not enough and a series of *Flakpanzer*, mostly based on the PzKpfw IV, were produced. Towards the end of the war some heavier AA pieces on the Panther tank chassis were planned, but none was produced.

The full inventory of self-propelled gun types in the Wehrmacht runs into three figures and it is not possible to describe every single type; moreover, some of them were single prototypes or built only in handfuls. Here, then, we look at the types of major importance only since these were the types in large scale service.

Waffenträger

Weapons carriers were unique to the German Army during the Second World War, and characteristic of the very advanced thinking which the German design engineers applied to military problems. The *Waffenträger* was a class not developed for the armoured forces, but evolved in the first place for the field artillery. Had developments been carried through to their logical conclusion and full scale production started, then almost the entire field army, as far as 'teeth' arms were concerned, would have been fully motorised and to a large degree fully armoured. The development history is quite distinct from that of self-propelled artillery and the functions of *Waffenträger*

SiG 33 SP infantry guns in an armoured column move up through a devastated Russian landscape

PzJg RSO
This *Panzerjäger* mounted a 75-mm Pak 40 on the chassis of the *Osttractor* artillery tractor

as originally foreseen were simply to facilitate the mobility of the artillery, not to fight in the armoured role.

In 1942, the Army's Artillery Branch, no doubt inspired by developments in the self-propelled gun field, put up proposals and requirements for a form of carriage which enabled the field artillery to carry out its traditional role, harnessing a tracked vehicle to replace the horse team or gun tractor. There was some evidence here of inter-branch controversy, for the artillerymen did not consider assault guns and similar self-propelled guns with limited traverse mounts to be fully suitable for a divisional artillery role, though they liked the mobility which these weapons enjoyed.

Detailed specifications were issued, and subsequently a large number of firms built prototypes. In fact, many *Waffenträger* types were projected but relatively few were actually made. The PzKpfw IV chassis was used for the 1942–43 designs, and two early projects which did not see fruition featured either a demountable 150-mm FH 18 or a 128-mm FH 81. These were very heavy pieces and the designs were probably dropped because of weight problems. The very first *Waffenträger* built was the *Heuschrecke* (Locust) IVb which, as the designation implies, was also on the Panzer IV chassis. This was fully designated GW IVb *für* 105-mm le FH 18/1 (chassis for the 105-mm light field howitzer 18/1).

A development of the *Heuschrecke* was the *Grille* (Cricket). Fully designated 105-mm le FH 18/40 *auf Fahrgestell* GW/III/IV (105-mm light field howitzer 18/40 on the chassis of gun carrier III/IV), this vehicle was on the running gear of the proposed PzKpfw III/IV.

What finally evolved were two standard chassis – a light weapons carrier (*leichter Waffenträger*) and a medium weapons carrier (*mittlerer Waffenträger*). Mechanically these two vehicles featured the running gear, steering transmission, and final drive of the original PzKpfw 38 (t) design.

Production of these standard *Waffenträger* was scheduled to begin in March 1945 and reach an output of 350 a month by late that year. Firms which had been involved in PzKpfw IV production were to switch over to building the new *Waffenträger* vehicles. Adding to these the *Hetzer* and the proposed *Schützenpanzerwagen* auf 38(t) it can be seen that a fully rationalised output of light armoured vehicles would be produced starting in 1945, which would replace dozens of older types of self-propelled weapon and the various half-tracks. Taking into account also the E series tanks and the projected Panther II, it is apparent that a completely new look Panzer Division was not far off – lean, streamlined and fully rationalised.

What was projected on paper, however, was far too late to stand a chance of realisation for while the plans were sound, the German war machine and the economy were fast collapsing in the early spring of 1945. By the time Germany surrendered, the only real progress with this new-look equipment was the prototypes, some jigs, and a lot of drawings. It is of interest to note, however, that what had started out as a rather esoteric artillery dream of fanciful vehicles which could emplace their own guns had turned by degrees into a highly sophisticated and ruthlessly standardised type of vehicle.

STURMGESCHÜTZ

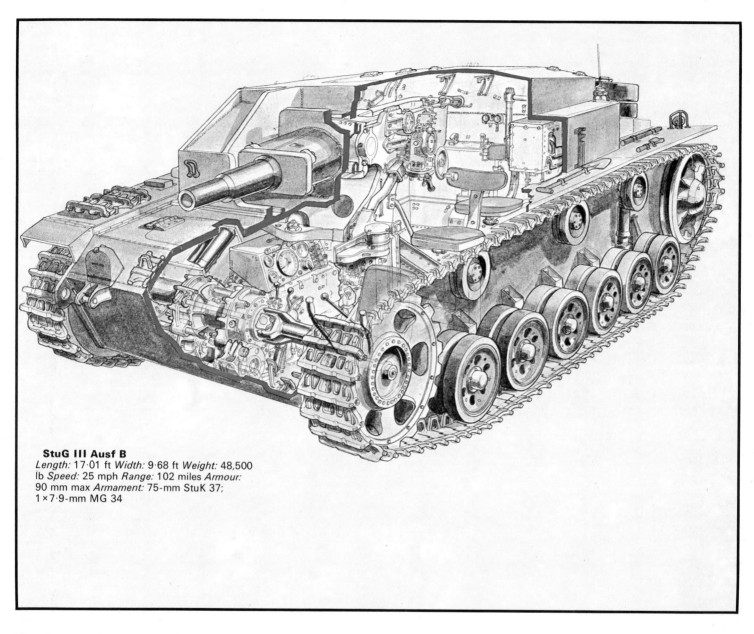

StuG III Ausf B
Length: 17·01 ft *Width:* 9·68 ft *Weight:* 48,500 lb *Speed:* 25 mph *Range:* 102 miles *Armour:* 90 mm max *Armament:* 75-mm StuK 37; 1 × 7·9-mm MG 34

The *Sturmgeschütz*, or assault gun, takes pride of place in the story of German self-propelled guns. The first steps to procure an assault gun go back to mid-1936, when *Heereswaffenamt* agreed to a request by the Inspector of Infantry's department for an armoured vehicle to provide supporting fire for the infantry.

Daimler were asked to prepare designs based on the Panzer III which was already going into production, and Krupp were asked to design the superstructure and armament. As finally drawn up, the vehicle, designated *Sturmgeschütz III*, was exactly like the current PzKpfw III A Ausf E mechanically and structurally up to track cover level, above which it had a low enveloping armoured superstructure in place of the usual turret, since a low silhouette was specially requested. Armament was the familiar 75-mm L/24 low velocity gun as fitted to the PzKpfw IV tank. Armour protection was 50 mm at the front, reducing to a minimum of 10 mm elsewhere. A pre-production batch of 30

vehicles was ordered in 1939 and the first of these were in service for the invasion of France, where they proved successful.

Lagging production

The original designation was *Gerpanzerte Selbstfahrlafette für Sturmgeschütz* 75-mm KwK (armoured carriage for 75-mm assault gun). A full production order was placed for the vehicle, deliveries to start in September 1940 and to proceed at the rate of 50 a month. Built on the by then current PzKpfw III Ausf F turret they were little different from the pre-production type, being designated SdKfz 142. The Maybach HL 120 TR engine with Maybach Variorex gearbox gave performance similar to that of the PzKpfw III tank, with ten forward speeds and one reverse. The empty weight was 20·2 tonnes and combat weight 22 tonnes. There was a crew of four and 44 rounds were carried. Built during the winter of 1940–41, some 184 vehicles of this type were completed. By this time of course production was already lagging behind

requirements and this marked the start of production of the improvised *Panzerjäger* and *Sturmhaubitze* types to keep up the numbers of vehicles in the field.

An improved engine and only detail changes marked the Ausf B, the third type to appear. Improved frontal armour was featured and 548 were built by the firm of Alkett. All these three variants were externally similar and are easily distinguished by the short L/24 gun.

However, the shape of things to come was shown in a new interim production model designated *Sturmgeschütz Lange* 75-mm *Kanone* L/33 (assault gun with long 75-mm gun L/33). This recognised the need for an anti-tank capability and featured a lengthened higher velocity version of the 75-mm weapon. Krupp and Alkett built these vehicles early in 1942, largely as a result of early experience on the Russian Front. The vehicle was unchanged from the Ausf B except for the new gun.

By now the Wehrmacht was fully involved in the Russian campaign and the vast

StuG III Ausf G, with 105-mm howitzer in place of the 75-mm gun, Zimmerit anti-magnetic paste and rails for Schürzen side plates. Inset, left: General Heinz Guderian, mastermind of the Panzer Divisions. Sacked after the German defeat at the battle of Moscow, he was later appointed Inspector of Armoured Forces, though a clerical error left 90% of self-propelled guns outside his terms of reference

numerical superiority of Soviet tanks made it imperative that the assault gun must now be fully capable of taking on tanks. As a result the long 75-mm StuK 40 L/43, as then being fitted to PzKpfw IVs was fitted in the mantlet of the *Sturmgeschütz* from February 1942. Some early vehicles had no muzzle brakes. Only 119 of these vehicles were built before production changed to a newer improved model. All these early vehicles had quite simple armour disposition with plain hatches, sighting window in the front superstructure, and an armoured radio box each side.

However, from June 1942, a much revised model was produced, resulting from an order given by Hitler at the end of 1941 after the Russian T-34 tank had been encountered for the first time. The new model was designated 75-mm *Sturmgeschütz* 40 Ausf G, having the even longer StuK 40 L/48 gun as standard and an improved superstructure with frontal armour increased to 80-mm thick. Built on the PzKpfw III Ausf G chassis, it continued to be produced unchanged until late in 1943. In later models the Ausf J, L and M chassis were used with consequent changes in appearance of sprocket wheel, idler and track width. This vehicle had an MG 34 with 600 rounds as standard, and an empty weight of 21·6 tonnes. An armoured commander's hatchway and revised superstructure were new features.

In 1943 the model was again improved, to be more commonly known as the *Sturmgeschütz* III Ausf G (StuG III Ausf G). Spaced frontal armour, a commander's cupola, and side skirts were featured. Later vehicles had a much improved cast *Saukopf* mantlet replacing the fabricated mantlet of earlier vehicles. Many were coated with the Zimmerit anti-magnetic paste, and a layer of concrete up to six inches deep was added to the armoured roof of the driving compartment. The final production vehicles were fitted with the *Nalwerteidgungswaffe* (close defence weapon), an internally loaded bomb thrower which projected anti-personnel and smoke charges against attacking infantry. A remote-control MG 34 was also by now standardised. This late production Ausf G had been built on the chassis of the late (10/ZW) PzKpfw III tank, and when Panzer III production ceased completely in August 1943, the chassis was produced solely for assault gun use. Some detail changes, eliminating non-essential fittings, were made to the chassis at this time. Over 9000 of the various production versions of the StuG III Ausf G had been built by the time the factories were captured by the Allies.

Support StuGs
Giving the StuG III an anti-tank capability detracted from its performance in the infantry support role, so an additional series of vehicles was built to support the StuG IIIs. These were simply StuG III Ausf G models with a 105-mm *Sturmhaubitze* 42 howitzer; consequently the type was designated 105-mm *Sturmhaubitze* 42 Ausf G. Some had the *Saukopf* mantlet and others the cast type; some lacked a muzzle brake. A few vehicles were unarmed and were used as munitions carriers for the assault guns, while others were used by engineers of tank battalions to carry bridging equipment. Racks were fitted on top of the superstructure to hold assault bridge sections. Over 1000 105-mm *Sturmhaubitze* 42 vehicles were built in 1943–45.

In 1942 one other type of assault gun on the PzKpfw III chassis was produced. This was the *Sturm-infanteriegeschütz* 33 *auf* PzKpfw III, which featured the 150-mm L/11 howitzer in a high armoured superstructure. A crew of five was provided and the vehicle weighed 22 tonnes. The idea of this vehicle was for use in close street fighting, and 12 were built for combat trials. Subsequently it was decided that heavier armour was required but the Panzer III chassis was not powerful enough to allow the extra weight needed, and the project was abandoned in favour of the *Brummbar* (Grizzly Bear) on the PzKpfw IV chassis. The 12 SiG 33s built saw service on the Russian Front.

Yet another version of the *Sturmgeschütz* saw service in larger numbers, however, the StuG IV, basically the same conversion as the StuG III, but on a Panzer IV chassis, with the difference in overall length made up by fabricating a new roof section. Some 632 StuG IVs were built, starting in mid-1943.

StuG III Ausf G with bolted box mantlet and Schürzen *advances through a maize field*

StuG III Ausf G
Length: 20·14 ft *Width:* 9·71 ft *Weight:*
52,690 lb *Speed:* 25 mph *Range:* 105 miles
Armour: 90 mm max *Armament:* 105-mm StuK 42;
1 x 7·92-mm MG 34

PANZERJÄGER

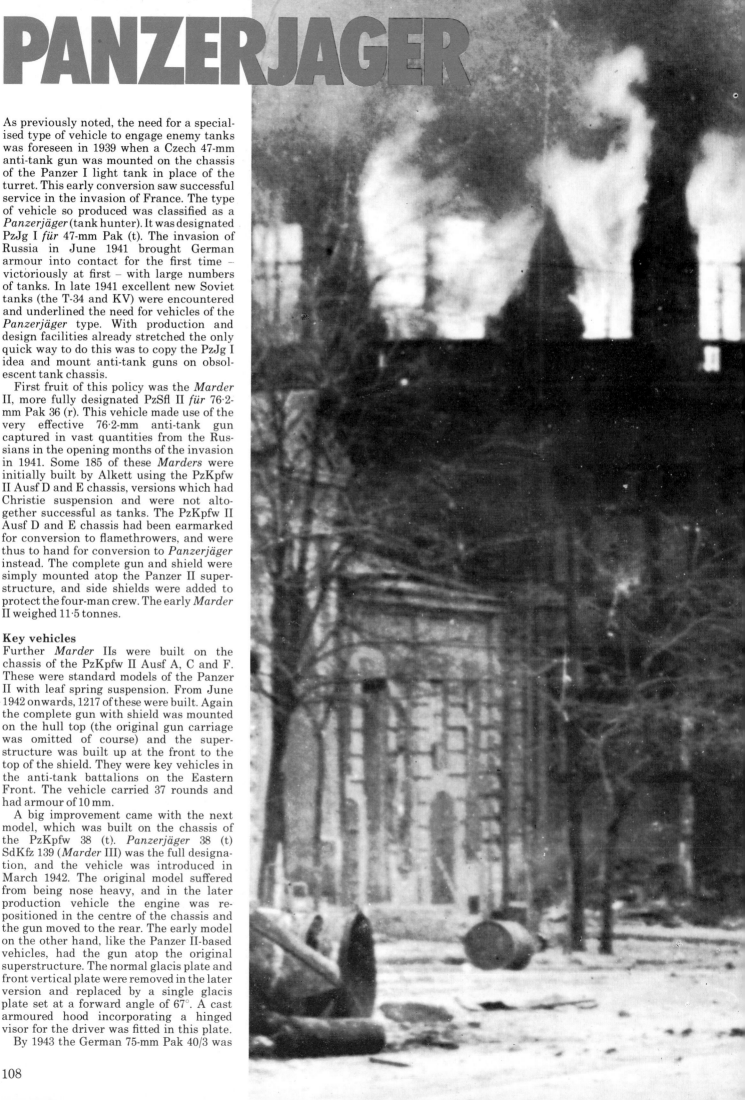

As previously noted, the need for a special-ised type of vehicle to engage enemy tanks was foreseen in 1939 when a Czech 47-mm anti-tank gun was mounted on the chassis of the Panzer I light tank in place of the turret. This early conversion saw successful service in the invasion of France. The type of vehicle so produced was classified as a *Panzerjäger* (tank hunter). It was designated PzJg I *für* 47-mm Pak (t). The invasion of Russia in June 1941 brought German armour into contact for the first time – victoriously at first – with large numbers of tanks. In late 1941 excellent new Soviet tanks (the T-34 and KV) were encountered and underlined the need for vehicles of the *Panzerjäger* type. With production and design facilities already stretched the only quick way to do this was to copy the PzJg I idea and mount anti-tank guns on obsol-escent tank chassis.

First fruit of this policy was the *Marder* II, more fully designated PzSfl II *für* 76·2-mm Pak 36 (r). This vehicle made use of the very effective 76·2-mm anti-tank gun captured in vast quantities from the Rus-sians in the opening months of the invasion in 1941. Some 185 of these *Marders* were initially built by Alkett using the PzKpfw II Ausf D and E chassis, versions which had Christie suspension and were not alto-gether successful as tanks. The PzKpfw II Ausf D and E chassis had been earmarked for conversion to flamethrowers, and were thus to hand for conversion to *Panzerjäger* instead. The complete gun and shield were simply mounted atop the Panzer II super-structure, and side shields were added to protect the four-man crew. The early *Marder* II weighed 11·5 tonnes.

Key vehicles

Further *Marder* IIs were built on the chassis of the PzKpfw II Ausf A, C and F. These were standard models of the Panzer II with leaf spring suspension. From June 1942 onwards, 1217 of these were built. Again the complete gun with shield was mounted on the hull top (the original gun carriage was omitted of course) and the super-structure was built up at the front to the top of the shield. They were key vehicles in the anti-tank battalions on the Eastern Front. The vehicle carried 37 rounds and had armour of 10 mm.

A big improvement came with the next model, which was built on the chassis of the PzKpfw 38 (t). *Panzerjäger* 38 (t) SdKfz 139 (*Marder* III) was the full designa-tion, and the vehicle was introduced in March 1942. The original model suffered from being nose heavy, and in the later production vehicle the engine was re-positioned in the centre of the chassis and the gun moved to the rear. The early model on the other hand, like the Panzer II-based vehicles, had the gun atop the original superstructure. The normal glacis plate and front vertical plate were removed in the later version and replaced by a single glacis plate set at a forward angle of 67°. A cast armoured hood incorporating a hinged visor for the driver was fitted in this plate.

By 1943 the German 75-mm Pak 40/3 was

Panzerjäger I
First of the long line of German specialised anti-tank SP mountings
Length: 14·51 ft *Width:* 5·07 ft *Weight:* 14,110 lb *Speed:* 25 mph *Range:* 87 miles *Armour:* 14 mm max *Armament:* 47-mm Pak(t)

A Panzerjäger I enters the blazing city of Rostov towards the end of the first phase of the battle for Russia, in November 1941

SdKfz 132 'Marder' II
A potent tank destroyer, the first 'marten'
mounted the captured Russian 76·2-mm anti-
tank gun on PzKpfw II Ausf D or E chassis

A heavily camouflaged Marder *II on the move*

available, and in the late *Marder* III it was mounted on a platform at pannier height and was shielded by a three-sided superstructure of 10-mm plate that extended over the tracks and to the extreme rear of the hull. This arrangement extended the fighting compartment more conveniently to the back of the hull. A support for the gun when in the travelling position was mounted on the front horizontal plate. About 750 early *Marder* III and 800 late *Marder* III were built. The gun could be traversed 30° left and right and elevated −10° to +25°, common for all various *Marder* models.

Marder I was entirely different in appearance, built on the chassis of the captured French Lorraine carrier which was taken into German service as a standard type, and used as the basis for several SP vehicles. *Marder* I, full designation *Panzerjäger für 75-mm Pak 40/1 (Sf) Lorraine Schlepper (f)*, ran to only 184 vehicles converted by the firm of Becker in 1942–43. These were all used in France, where they first saw action in the battle of Normandy in 1944. The Lorraine carrier was a very stable tracked munitions and personnel carrier taken over in large numbers when France capitulated. It had a flat load space which lent itself admirably to conversion to a gun carriage and formed a basis for several improvised types.

While the *Marder* series were the most standardised and numerous of the improvised *Panzerjäger* types, there were many others, large and small. Of major importance was the *Nashorn* (Rhinoceros) or *Hornisse* (Hornet) which was fully designated 88-mm Pak 43/1 *auf Fgst* PzKpfw III/IV, later *Panzerjäger* III/IV. As its designation implies, its chassis was a combination of Panzer III and Panzer IV components. The powerful 88-mm Pak 43 was put on a mobile mount as soon as production guns were available in 1943. Some 473 *Nashorns* were built. The open superstructure was only lightly armoured due to the weight of the gun, which rather overloaded the chassis, and production ceased as improved *Jagdpanzer* types became available.

Most of the other *Panzerjäger* types were small and relatively unimportant. Among them were the 37-mm Pak 35/6 on infantry

'Marder' I
This type of *Panzerjäger* mounted the 75-mm Pak 40/1 on the captured *Lorraine Schlepper*

SdKfz 138 'Marder' III
A late model *Marder* III, with the fighting compartment extended to the back of the hull
Length: 15·26 ft *Width:* 7·09 ft *Weight:* 23,150 lb *Speed:* 26 mph *Range:* 115 miles *Armour:* 25 mm max *Armament:* 75-mm Pak 40/3

carrier chassis such as the French VE and the ex-British Bren or Universal carrier (these were captured at Dunkirk). The ex-French Renault R-35 and Hotchkiss H-39 tanks were fitted with the 47-mm Czech gun and the Pak 40 to give *Marder*-like vehicles; these were used mainly by the occupying forces in France and fought in the Normandy campaign. An unusual conversion in the same vein featured a Hotchkiss 20-mm anti-tank gun mounted in a shield on a captured British Matilda tank, and some of these were used by occupying troops in Denmark, France and the Low Countries.

When the *Raupenschlepper* (Eastfront tracked tractor) appeared in 1943, 83 of them were converted to unarmoured *Panzerjäger* and entered service in 1944 as the 75-mm

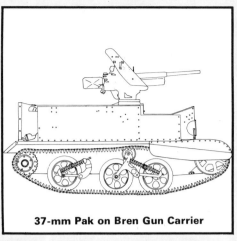

37-mm Pak on Bren Gun Carrier

Pak 40/1 auf RSO (Sf1). The Pak 40 gun was a field anti-tank piece less carriage mounted on a turntable on the load compartment. A canvas tilt was provided which served to disguise the vehicles true nature when it was rigged. Biggest of all these *Panzerjäger* types was the *Panzerjäger* 128-mm *Kanone* Sf VK 3001 (H) which was built on the chassis of one of the Henschel 30-ton prototypes which appeared during the development of the Tiger tank. This prototype tank was discarded in 1941 when 45-ton prototypes were called for. Two of the four VK 3001 (H) chassis completed were converted to very heavy *Panzerjäger* with the massive 128-mm K 40 as an anti-tank weapon against heavy tanks. An open top superstructure with rear door was fitted.

SdKfz 164 'Hornisse'
Also known as 'rhinoceros' the 'hornet' mounted the powerful 88-mm Pak 43 on the PzKpfw III/IV chassis

47-mm Pak 40 on Renault R-35
One of many minor *Panzerjäger* conversions on captured foreign vehicles

JAGDPANZER

The *Jagdpanzer* (hunting tank) was a natural development from both the *Sturmgeschütz* and *Panzerjäger* types and exhibited characteristics of both. The interim designs of 1943 mostly carried two designations, one as a *Panzerjäger* and another as a *Jagdpanzer*.

The classic example of this was the massive *Elefant* (originally *Ferdinand*, after its designer, Ferdinand Porsche), which was one of the most famous of all German AFVs. The original designation was PzJg Tiger (P) *Ferdinand für 88-mm Pak 43/2* and this was subsequently changed to *Jagdpanzer Elefant für 88-mm Pak 43/2 L/71* (SdKfz 184). It was decided to alter the uncompleted Porsche Tigers rejected in favour of the Henschel models, to make a self-propelled mount for the 88-mm Pak 43.

The *Elefant* was a complete re-design of the original Porsche project – virtually a new vehicle. Only the suspension and hull shape of the original Porsche Tiger remained. The original petrol-electric drive was retained, but was modified in that the Porsche air-cooled drive motors were replaced by two Maybach 300 hp HL 120 engines. These were centrally sited instead of being located at the rear, leaving the rear hull available for the fighting compartment. Drive was to the rear sprocket.

The driver and radio-operator sat in the hull front forward of the engines, the driver having a hydropneumatic steering system. Fuel tanks flanked the central engine compartment and the rear was given over to a full-width, slope-sided fighting compartment, which housed the commander, gunner and two loaders.

The *Elefant's* punch

The punch of the *Elefant* was its 88-mm Pak 43/2 L/71, a later development of the 88-mm Flak 36 which had been adapted as a weapon for the Tiger tanks. This was a more powerful (and longer) gun than the earlier 88-mm weapons. Originally the 88-mm gun was the only armament, but early combat experience showed that close range armament was necessary to prevent infantrymen from attacking the vehicle. Hence, a machine-gun was added in the front hull.

Vision from the *Elefant* was poor – forward only – so cupolas were added, and appliqué armour was extensively added in bolt-on form, with 100 mm added to the nose and 200 mm on the superstructure front. Elsewhere the armour thickness was up to 80 mm. There was a large circular hatch in the superstructure rear for weapons maintenance and this featured a smaller hatch for ejecting spare cartridges. Other superstructure apertures were pistol ports and two roof hatches. The Porsche suspension was novel, consisting of three twin bogies on each side sprung by torsion bars. The wheels were all steel with resilient rims.

The prototype *Elefant* appeared in March 1943, and in July that year the *Elefants*, by now allocated to Panzer Regiment 654, were used for the first time in action with disastrous results. Still mechanically unreliable, many broke down, became bogged down or were over-run and captured by infantry at close quarters. Their use was then restricted and most of the survivors found their way to Italy in 1944, where many were lost to Allied tanks.

Developed from the StuG III and IV was a much refined design specially for tank destroying, and this vehicle, the *Jagdpanzer* IV, was the first true *Jagdpanzer* designed as such. Designated *Jagdpanzer* IV Ausf F (75-mm Pak 39 L/48) SdKfz 162, it was first in service late in 1943. It incorporated all the lessons learned from the use of the StuG III in the anti-tank role. Sloped armour with a very low silhouette was a distinctive feature, and the vehicle had 60 mm thick upper and lower frontal armour, well-sloped for optimum shot deflection. The sloping superstructure sides were carried over the full track width to give increased ammunition stowage, compared with the StuG III, of 79 rounds. The top of the superstructure was in one piece, with two hatches, and there was another small hatch through which a dial sight could be extended. Spaced armour was carried on each side of the superstructure.

The main armament of one 75-mm Pak 39 was mounted in the sloping superstructure front, the mount being of gimbal type protected by an external cast mantlet. Elevation limits were −8° to +10°, with traverse 12° left and 10° right. The gun fired APBC (Armour-Piercing Ballistic Cap) ammunition at a muzzle velocity of 2300 fps, or HE shells at 1800 fps. Hollow charge rounds, AP 40 shot and smoke could also be fired, making the vehicle very versatile and effective. Early models had rounded front plates and late ones lacked a muzzle-brake on the gun. In late 1944 a revised model appeared with all-steel wheels (dispensing with rubber tyres) and an improved StuK 42 75-mm L/70, known as the *Jagdpanzer* IV/70. These vehicles were first-line equipment until the end of the war.

The finest *Jagdpanzer* of all, however, was the splendid and impressive *Jagdpanther*, the most important derivative of the Panther tank and another of the classic wartime AFVs. Both the *Elefant* and the *Nashorn* had been built as *Panzerjäger* types, as already described, but neither of these was satisfactory.

The need for a fast, up-to-date tank destroyer on a modern chassis was met by adapting the Panther as the previous attempts to produce a heavy tank destroyer had been so unsuccessful. The 88-mm Pak 43 had been mounted on the Porsche Tiger chassis (to make the *Ferdinand*) and on the PzKpfw III/IV chassis as the *Nashorn*, but both of these improvisations proved unsatisfactory: *Ferdinand* was too heavy and *Nashorn* too small and under-powered.

By 1943, however, there was an urgent need for tank destroyers in quantity so it was decided to utilise the best available chassis, that of the Panther. MIAG were asked to work out the design and the prototype was first demonstrated, in the presence of Hitler, on 20 October 1943. The Panther chassis was used unaltered, but the front and upper side plates were extended upwards to make a well-sloped enclosed

Jagdpanzer IV, mounting the 75-mm StuK 40 on the PzKpfw IV chassis, the first true Jagdpanzer

JgPz V Jagdpanther
Best of all the 'hunting tanks' the *Jagdpanther* was one of the all-time classic fighting vehicles
Length: 32·35 ft *Width:* 10·76 ft *Weight:* 95,900 lb *Speed:* 29 mph *Range:* 130 miles
Armour: 80 mm max *Armament:* 88-mm Pak 43/3; 2×7·92-mm MG 34

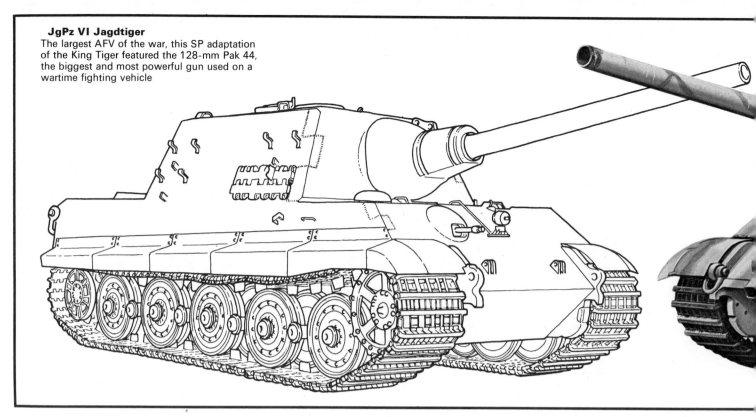

JgPz VI Jagdtiger
The largest AFV of the war, this SP adaptation of the King Tiger featured the 128-mm Pak 44, the biggest and most powerful gun used on a wartime fighting vehicle

superstructure. The mantlet was fitted in the centre of the hull front with a limited traverse for the 88-mm Pak 43/3 L/71 gun of 11° each side. Armour was 80 mm in front and 60 mm at the sides. A ball-mounted MG 34 was fitted in the right front of the hull and the driver sat in the usual position in the left front. Sighting equipment consisted of a rangefinder and periscope telescope. The telescope protruded through a slot in the roof within an armoured quadrant arc linked to the gun mount.

The new SP version of the Panther was at first designated 88-mm Pak 43/3 *auf Panzerjäger* Panther (SdKfz 173) but at Hitler's personal suggestion in February 1944 it was redesignated simply as the *Jagdpanther* (Hunting Panther).

MIAG commenced building *Jagdpanther* in February 1944, using the Ausf G chassis which had by then become the current production type. By the war's end 382 had been completed. First production *Jagdpanthers* had a one-piece barrel, but later a two-piece barrel was used on the 88-mm weapon to ease barrel changing, as the barrel did not wear uniformly and it was economical to make in it two parts. Later *Jagdpanthers* had a simplified collar round a thicker, bolted mantlet.

Crew of the *Jagdpanther* consisted of a commander, gunner, two loaders, radio-operator/machine-gunner and driver. The vehicle carried 60 88-mm rounds. The *Jagdpanther* was the best and most potent of all the German tank destroyers. It was well-shaped, low, fast and heavily armoured. It was intended to build *Jagdpanther* at a rate of 150 per month, but disrupted production facilities in the last year of the war made this target quite impossible.

Following *Heereswaffenamt* policy, a limited traverse tank hunter version of the King Tiger tank was also produced. This vehicle, originally designated *Panzerjäger* Tiger Ausf B (SdKfz 186), consisted essentially of the King Tiger hull with a box-like superstructure holding a 128-mm Pak 44 L/55 gun, the largest gun installed in any wartime AFV. An unarmoured full-size

Length: 32·35 ft Width: 10·76 ft Weight: 158,000 lb Speed: 24 mph Range: 105 miles Armour: 250 mm max Armament: 128-mm Pak 44; 1 × 7·92-mm MG 34

JgPz 38(t) 'Hetzer'
The 'baiter', a light *Jagdpanzer* using the ubiquitous PzKpfw 38(t) chassis first appeared in mid-1941. Its armour disposition, concentrated around the hull and turret front, is shown

Length: 20·57 ft Width: 8·63 ft Weight: 35,275 lb Speed: 26 mph Range: 110 miles Armour: 60 mm max Armament: 75-mm Pak 39; 1 × 7·92-mm MG 42

mock-up of the new vehicle was completed in October 1942 at the same time as the prototype King Tiger. At 76 tons the *Jagdtiger* was the largest fighting vehicle to see action during the war.

Henschel co-operated with Krupp in the design of the gun mount, which featured the small *Saukopf* mantlet. To utilise internal stowage to the best advantage, separate ammunition was used with the 128-mm gun, and to assist with carrying the added weight the suspension was spaced out by an extra 260 mm. A total of 150 *Panzerjäger* Tiger Bs were ordered and they were built by Steyr-Daimler-Puch at St Valentin in Austria. In the event, shortages and disruptions meant that only 70 vehicles were built, 48 of them in 1944. Initially there was an interruption in the supply of the 128-mm gun and it was proposed to overcome this by installing the same 88-mm gun as in the *Jagdpanther*. In February 1944, on Hitler's orders, the name of the vehicle was simplified (in common with other types) and it was called the *Jagdtiger*, the designation by which it is best remembered.

Dr Porsche attempted to improve on the design by installing torsion bar bogie suspension, similar to that used on the prototype Tiger and the *Elefant*. One vehicle was converted to this standard, and Porsche claimed that production was greatly simplified. However, the urgent need for tanks did not allow time for changes to be made and any possible slight advantage of the Porsche suspension did not justify the added time lag. Externally this vehicle was distinguished by having one less road wheel each side.

Jagdtiger saw service from late 1944 until the end of the war, but although a most formidable weapon, it demonstrated that the tactical limitations of such large, heavy vehicles became a liability, even in the defensive type of warfare the panzers were then fighting. Even the lighter King Tiger strained logistic and tactical resources, and the lumbering *Jagdtiger*, a large, slow-moving target, subject to frequent breakdowns, was in no way a success. It remains an impressive engineering achievement, however, and is assured of its place in AFV history by virtue of its immense size and firepower.

Hetzer

In March 1943 it was also decided to build a light *Jagdpanzer*, and the ever reliable PzKpfw 38(t) chassis was called upon. What amounted to a miniature version of the *Jagdpanther* was produced. The vehicle was fitted with the 75-mm KwK 40 L/48 gun and designated *Jagdpanzer* 38(t) *Hetzer*. The first models appeared in May 1944 and all subsequent PzKpfw 38(t) production was diverted to build *Hetzer*. Over 1500 had been built by the end of the war and the vehicle was highly successful. A number were completed as flame-throwers, with a flame projector replacing the gun. Frontal armour was 60 mm, all plates were well sloped and the vehicle weighed 16 tonnes. A remote-control MG 42 was fitted in the roof for close-in defence.

The PzKpfw 38(t) chassis was so good that it was chosen to form the basis for a whole new series of light armoured vehicles. A *Panzerjäger Kanone* with 75-mm L/70 gun was planned in 1945, but never produced. The chassis for the new standard series was designated 38 (d).

PANZERARTILLERIE

SiG 33s: 150-mm infantry assault guns on PzKpfw I Ausf B chassis

150-mm SiG 33 auf PzKpfw III
Length: 15·58 ft *Width:* 7·34 ft *Weight:* 26,455
lb *Speed:* 25 mph *Range:* 124 miles *Armour:*
20 mm max *Armament:* 150-mm SiG 33

150-mm SiG 33 auf PzKpfw II

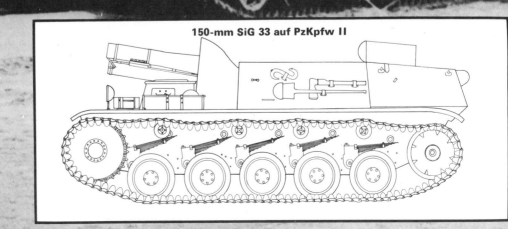

SdKfz 124 'Wespe'
The 'wasp' conversion of a PzKpfw II ausf H
Length: 15·72 ft *Width:* 7·35 ft *Weight:* 25,350
lb *Speed:* 25 mph *Range:* 87 miles *Armour:* 90
mm max *Armament:* 105-mm PzFH

Hummel (bumble bee), featuring a 150-mm
gun on the hybrid PzKpfw III/IV chassis

The classification *Panzerartillerie* covers self-propelled equipment which gave fire support in the field but was not used in an anti-tank role: *Infanterie Geschütze* (infantry guns), *Sturmhaubitze* (assault howitzers), *Panzerhaubitze* (armoured howitzers) and so on. Many of these had foreign chassis and the types were diverse.

The first was the much over-loaded 150-mm SiG 33 4/12 auf PzKpfw I of 1940, which, like the PzJg I, proved the value of this type of mobile artillery. The Panzer II proved a more stable and suitable carriage for the 150-mm gun and many had entered service by 1942, serving with particular success in the Western Desert. Designated 150-mm SiG 33 L/12 auf Fgst PzKpfw II (sf), it came in two forms, one on the unaltered chassis and one on an extended chassis with an extra wheel each side. The superstructure was open with low sides; the vehicle weighed 10 tonnes.

Yet another infantry gun model was the 150-mm SiG 33 (Shl) auf PzKpfw 38 (t) *Bison*, an extremely crude 1942 adaptation which was replaced by a 1943–44 version in which the engine was moved forward into the original fighting compartment and the gun and superstructure were moved to the rear. This made for a better balanced vehicle. About 370 of both types were built.

Much more successful was the 150-mm *Panzerhaubitze* 18/1 auf PzKpfw III/IV *Hummel* (Bumble Bee) which was a *Panzer-*

artillerie equivalent to the *Nashorn*. Built on the PzKpfw III/IV chassis, this was produced from late 1942 until the end of the war, and over 660 were built. Weight was 26 tonnes and there was a five-man crew. The *Hummel* had the long 150-mm gun rather than the infantry gun.

One of the best conversions was the 150-mm SFH 13/1 auf GW *Lorraine Schlepper* (t). The gun was an obsolete Krupp piece of 1917 which was adapted and fitted to the Lorraine chassis by the firm of Becker of Krefeld. The mounting of this quite heavy weapon rather overloaded the suspension, but it was popular and effective, and the conversion was quickly carried out. This 8·3-tonne vehicle was used on all fronts and first served widely with the Afrika Korps in 1942. It was in service up to the end of the war.

The most important of all *Panzerartillerie* vehicles was probably the *Wespe* (Wasp), designated fully as le FH 18/2 *auf* Fgst PzKpfw II (sE) (light field howitzer 18/2 on carriage of the PzKpfw II tank) which went into production in 1942 and continued until the end of the war.

By the last quarter of 1942 the Russian Front situation was stable enough to allow the design of more suitable *Panzerartillerie* conversions. The PzKpfw II Ausf F was selected for carrying the 105-mm light field gun. The design was ordered and by December 1942 the first *Wespen* were leaving the Famo assembly plant at Warsaw.

In February 1943 Hitler ordered that the total production capacity of the Panzer II be diverted to this purpose and that of the PzKpfw 38(t) to carrying the anti-tank guns. His reasons appear to have been the popularity of the first vehicles in service and an early attempt at standardisation, but most of all, the fact that the newly introduced hollow charge ammunition for artillery weapons would in time supplant the conventional anti-tank guns. So, by April 1943, only *Wespen* were appearing on the PzKpfw II chassis. Due to the war situation, production ceased in mid-1944, but by then 682 had been built and a further 158 without main armament were supplied as *Munitions-Selbstfahrlafette auf* PzKpfw II. This was because the *Wespe* could carry only 32 rounds and a munition carrier was needed to supply each battery. Generally, Wasps served with the Panzer or Panzer Grenadier Divisions in batteries of six, with between two and five batteries to a division.

The 105-mm le FH 18 was similarly fitted to the *Lorraine Schlepper*, and 24 were converted under the designation 105-mm le FH 18 auf GW *Lorraine Schlepper* (t). Forty-eight Hotchkiss H-39 tank chassis, 24 FCM tank chassis and a few Char B2s were given a similar conversion, and all these French vehicles served the occupying troops in France and saw combat in the Normandy fighting. There were also several other field howitzer vehicles of a minor nature.

Yet another conversion of a foreign tank, the 105-mm light field howitzer on the Lorraine Schlepper

105-mm Light Field Howitzer on Char B1 bis
A conversion of the captured French tank provided a makeshift SP gun

STURMPANZER

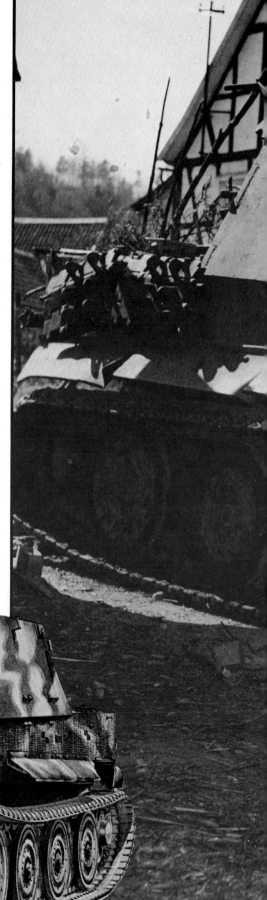

The last major types were the *Sturmpanzer* (assault tank) class, of which the most famous was the *Sturmpanzer* IV *Brummbar* (Grizzly Bear). Over 40 were built in 1943–44, specifically for street fighting on the Eastern Front. Very heavily armoured, the *Brummbar* weighed 28 tonnes and had 100 mm of front armour, and with a *Sturmhaubitze* 43 low velocity gun in an armoured mantlet it was a massive looking vehicle. Later examples had an added ball-mounted MG 34 in the hull front for self-defence. By the time the vehicle had been developed street fighting in Russian cities was a thing of the past, but *Brummbar* was a spectacular and formidable vehicle, difficult to knock out and living up to its name.

Even more formidable, however, was the heftiest of all, the *Sturmtiger*. Also known as the *Sturmpanzer* VI or *Sturmmörser*, this weapon was developed to requirements from the German Army engaged in the heavy street fighting at Stalingrad and other similar places in Russia. The full designation was 380-mm RW 61 Auf StuMrs *Tiger* (380-mm rocket projector Type 61 on Tiger chassis). The design owed its origins to a request for a self-propelled 210-mm howitzer capable of following up the advancing German troops and able to engage difficult targets with high angle fire. Hitler was personally responsible for instigating the idea for the weapon.

When development work started on the project, it was decided that the then-new PzKpfw VI Tiger Ausf E chassis would be used, but it was found that no suitable 210-mm gun was available. It was finally proposed to use the *Raketenwerfer* 61 L/54, a weapon that had originally been developed by the firm of Rheinmetall-Borsig as an anti-submarine device for the German Navy.

A model of the *Sturmtiger* was first shown on 20 October 1943, and the type went into limited production in August 1944, when ten existing Tiger tanks were converted by the firm of Alkett. For their intended role as mobile assault howitzers against troop concentrations and fortifications, they were heavily armoured. The suspension, power train, engine and hull were those of the basic Tiger E, but the normal superstructure and turret of the tank was replaced by a heavy rectangular superstructure. The welded superstructure was made of rolled armour plates, and the side plates were interlocked with the front and rear plates. A heavy strip of armour reinforced the joint between the front plate and glacis plate on the outside.

The rocket projector, mounted offset to the right of centre in the front plate of the rectangular superstructure, consisted of a tubular casting and spaced rifled liner and cast mantlet. The mantlet, an integral part of the tube, protected the joint of the tube and mount. Gases were deflected between the tube and liner and escaped through a perforated ring at the muzzle end. A rectangular loading hatch was located in the centre rear of the top plate and was closed by two doors, one forward and one to the rear. The rear door, spring balanced and hinged to open outwards, could be opened independently of the forward door and mounted a smoke projector. A small crane for loading the rocket projectiles was mounted on the superstructure.

Six ammunition racks on each side of the fighting compartment were provided within the vehicle to accommodate a total of 12 rounds, while an additional round could be carried in the projector tube. The rounds were of HE and Hollow Charge type. The 380-mm (15-in) HE projectile (380-mm R *Sprenggranat* 4581) had an overall length cf 56 in, a total weight of 761 lb and a maximum range of 6200 yards.

Sturmpanzer VI Sturmtiger
Length: 20·7 ft *Width:* 12·25 ft *Weight:* 156,800 lb *Speed:* 25 mph *Range:* 87 miles *Armour:* 6 in max *Armament:* 380-mm rocket projector; 1 × 7·92-mm MG 34

FLAKPANZER

Tanks specially adapted for the anti-aircraft role did not come into service until 1943 when the menace from Allied aircraft was becoming critical. The PzKpfw IV was the obvious choice for the major production models because of its stability as a gun platform, its size and its availability. The various models were produced quickly and the conversions were simple, an existing AA mount placed above the original turret space.

First off was the *Flakpanzer* IV (20-mm *Flakvierling* 38) *Möbelwagen* (furniture van). This simply had the *Flakvierling* 38 quadruple mount on its turntable, with hinged 10-mm armour sides which were lowered to give a 360° traverse for the mount. This was built on the PzKpfw IV Ausf H or S chassis, and over 200 were converted from standard tanks.

First of the Flakpanzer *was* Möbelwagen, *a quadruple 20-mm Flak 38 on PzKpfw chassis, with hinged armoured sides*

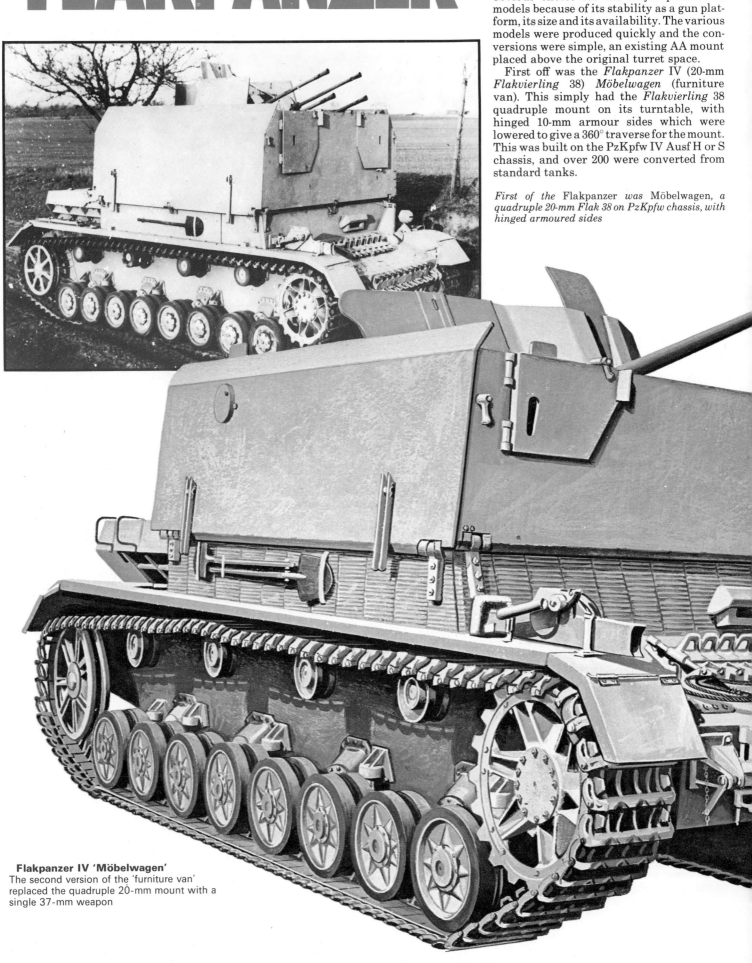

Flakpanzer IV 'Möbelwagen'
The second version of the 'furniture van' replaced the quadruple 20-mm mount with a single 37-mm weapon

A further variant was the *Flakpanzer* IV (37-mm Flak 43 L/60) *Möbelwagen* which was similar to the other *Möbelwagen* except that a single 37-mm mount replaced the *Flakvierling* 38.

Also developed late in 1943 was the *Flakpanzer* IV (20-mm) *mit* PzFGst Panzer IV/3 *Wirbelwind* (whirlwind) which was simply a basic PzKpfw IV Ausf J chassis with a 20-mm *Flakvierling* 38 quadruple mount in a multi-sided light armoured (10-mm) turret with 360° traverse. Over 340 were built during 1944 by the firm of Ostban. A few are believed to have been built on the PzKpfw III chassis.

Its counterpart with 37-mm single gun was *Flakpanzer* IV (37-mm) *Ostwind* (east wind) which was exactly like *Wirbelwind* except for the single 37-mm gun replacing

the quadruple mount. Deutsche Eisenwerke built 205 of these vehicles in 1944–45, converting them from PzKpfw IV Ausf J. An improved model with a later version of the 37-mm gun, in prototype stage at the end of the war was designated *Ostwind* II.

By 1945 a much improved *Flakpanzer*, designated *Leichter Flakpanzer* IV (30-mm) *Kugelblitz* (ball lightning) was at testing stage, but only five were built. The *Kugelblitz* had a fast-traversing power-operated turret with twin machine cannon MK 103/38 30-mm weapons. The guns had 80° maximum elevation. A further variant of this, *Zerstorer* 45 (destroyer 45) was at prototype stage by the end of the war. It had four 30-mm MK 103/38 guns and would have been a formidable machine had its development not been curtailed.

On the Russian Front a very simple vehicle, *Flakpanzer* 38 (t) was built to counter low flying Sturmovik aircraft. This was essentially the PzKpfw 38 (t) in its basic gun carriage form (as used for the *Marder* III) but with a single 20-mm Flak gun mounted. Over 160 of these were produced in the 1943–44 period.

The only other Flak vehicles akin to *Flakpanzer* were two experimental types on the *Grille* prototype *Waffenträger* chassis. They featured the 88-mm Flak 37 and 88-mm Flak 41 respectively in a mount with folding shields rather like the *Möbelwagen*. There were no production plans for these costly and heavy vehicles, however, and they appear to have been made by Krupp solely to make use of the available chassis which would otherwise have been discarded.

Flakpanzer IV 'Ostwind'

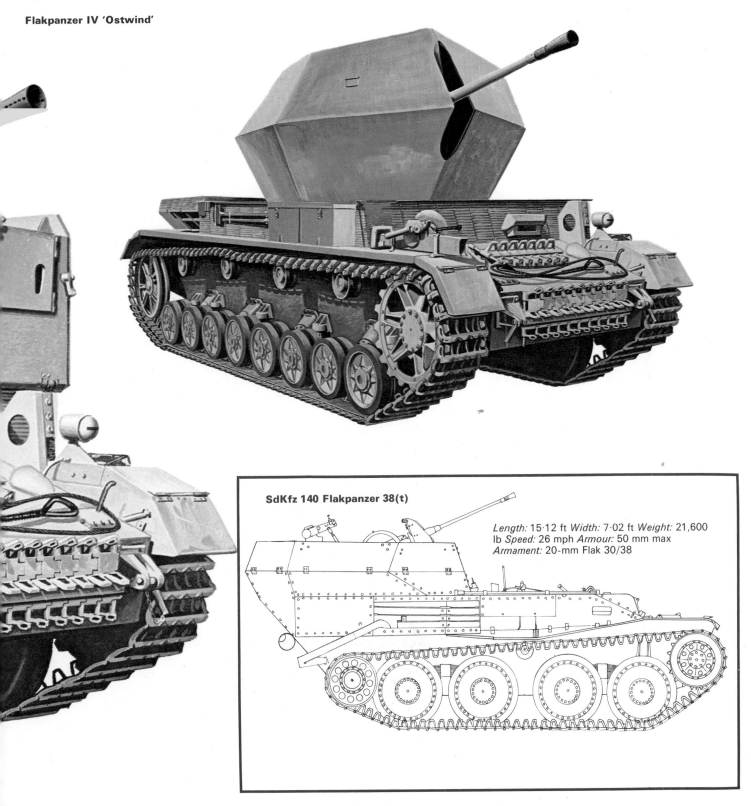

SdKfz 140 Flakpanzer 38(t)

Length: 15·12 ft *Width:* 7·02 ft *Weight:* 21,600 lb *Speed:* 26 mph *Armour:* 50 mm max *Armament:* 20-mm Flak 30/38

THE GIANT GUNS

600-mm Mortar 'Karl' (below and opposite)
Length: 36·58 ft *Width:* 10·33 ft *Weight:*
264,455 lb *Speed:* 6 mph *Armour:* 15 mm
Armament: 600-mm 040 mortar

Bundesarchiv

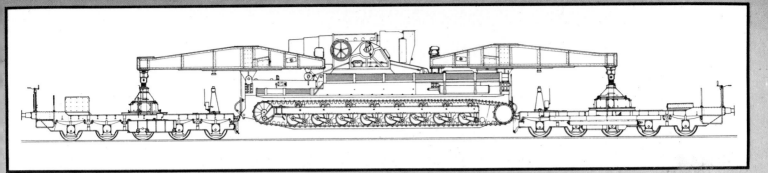

The largest tracked vehicles of all were the huge 600-mm mortars which were projected before the war. These might best be described as motorised tracked gun carriages. They were not Panzer Division vehicles and were in fact classified as siege artillery, but were actually self-propelled carriages with driving compartments. The first vehicle was built by Rheinmetall in 1939, under the designation 600-mm *Mörser Karl* (*Gerät* 040), and was intended to bombard the massively defended forts of the Maginot Line on the Franco-German border. The vehicle weighed 120 tonnes, was 11·15 metres long, and had 12-mm armour plate. The vehicle had a top speed of 6 mph. A second vehicle was built, designated 600-mm *Mörser Karl* II. By the time the two vehicles were in service France had fallen. Named *Thor* and *Eva*, the two pieces saw service on the Eastern Front and were particularly successful in the siege of Sevastopol in 1942, and also at Brest-Litovsk.

In 1943, as a result of these operations, six improved vehicles were ordered, designated 540-mm *Mörser Karl* (*Gerät* 041). The mortar was of different calibre, but it was generally similar to the original vehicle and weighed 130 tonnes.

To support these huge mortars, a special series of *Munitionspanzerwagen* IV was produced, based on the PzKpfw IV Ausf F. This type had a compartment for three rounds, and a 3·5-tonne crane lifted the round to mortar carriage. On the carriage itself the weapon detachment worked from platforms above the tracks. These platforms folded up alongside the carriage when the vehicle was on the move.

'Karl' being readied to hurl its 600-mm shell in a plunging arc towards Sevastopol. The piece could move short distances under its own power, but was slung between two rail bogies for longer journeys. Also shown is the Munitionenspanzerwagen *IV special ammunition carrier*